AN AMERICAN NUN IN TAIWAN

AN AMERICAN NUN
IN TAIWAN

Sister Mary Paul
with
C. Edmund Fisher

1967
DOUBLEDAY & COMPANY, INC., GARDEN CITY, NEW YORK

Nihil obstat: Reverend Paul Suen, M.A.

Imprimatur: ✠ Most Reverend Thomas Niu, D.D.
              Bishop of Yangku, China
              Apostolic Administrator—Chiayi Diocese
              Taiwan, Free China
              June 9, 1966

The *nihil obstat* and *imprimatur* are official declarations that a book or pamphlet is free of doctrinal or moral error. No implication is contained therein that those who have granted the *nihil obstat* and *imprimatur* agree with the contents, opinions or statements expressed.

AN AMERICAN NUN IN TAIWAN

Taiwan's northern port of Keelung, roughly shaped like a lobster claw, appeared in the early morning mist and low, black clouds. The date was November 26, 1959. I was so happy that I almost cried. Here, at last, was the realization of a fifteen-year-long dream of going to China, living Chinese and being Chinese among the Chinese. True, the upheaval caused by Communism after World War II changed my plans. Instead of Communist-occupied China, less than fifteen minutes away by jet airliner, my destination was Taiwan, the temporary outpost of the Free Republic of China. For the moment, I was too bubbly with enthusiasm to care about global politics. I itched to get off the Chinese freighter *Hai-min*, put my feet on Taiwan (400 years before, Portuguese sailors called it *Ihla Formosa*, Beautiful Island), and melt into the lives and culture of the Chinese people. My hands gripped the portside railing. I wanted to shout, "Hello to all of you; I am the luckiest girl in the world!" I was twenty-seven years old and full of adventure.

Then, all of a sudden, I was scared. I had never been abroad, and here I was a stranger in a strange country with vastly different customs, food and culture from those with which I had grown up back in Illinois. Also, all around me was the excited but incomprehensible babble of Chinese as my fellow passengers, all of them going home from the United States, pointed and waved at groups of people looming larger as the freighter edged toward dockside. I did not know the language. All I did know was how to use chopsticks.

I wondered what was behind those formidable mountains rising back of the shoreline, and how much of a journey it would be to my final destination, the Sisters of Our Lady of China community in a place called Chiayi-something-or-other. I wondered what the sisters would be like. Would they be ominous, like the clouds that threatened to unload their wrath in the form of drenching rain before the customs men finished checking our luggage on the open deck? With some exceptions, I had never felt close—really fully at ease—with sisters back in the United States; they seemed forbidding. And now I could not understand why I had chosen a community of Chinese sisters to work with as a lay missionary in the field of medicine. I wondered, too, about the people in the villages and cities? Would they accept me? And how about the food? Aboard ship it was delicious, but there were hints among the passengers that things were entirely different in the rural areas. I had a feeling that they were trying, in the typically Chinese polite manner, to tell me that I would find life very rugged in this place called Chiayi as opposed to the air-conditioned comforts and roast beef and steak diet back home. (The Chinese firmly believe that all Americans live luxuriously and dine sumptuously.)

I was to find out within twenty-four hours that life was not as easy as in the States. There was poverty in the Chiayi area. Not just among the people, but right inside the Our Lady of China community itself. In all frankness, I was totally unprepared for the rugged life that hit me, even during a stopover on that first night in Taiwan. There was a hard pallet that "broke" my back, and an equally hard rice-skin pillow that kinked my neck. Outside the netting over the pallet, mosquitoes swarmed and probed for a passageway. They wanted to feast on this "rich" American. Although they did not dine that night, their kinfolk banqueted later on elsewhere. Overhead, on the low-hanging, cardboard ceiling, a black, furry spider, the size of a silver dollar, glowered an eyeball-to-eyeball welcome. Shortly, I became positive that snakes would slither from holes in the mud walls. None did, fortunately, that night; they appeared some months later in what was mistakenly called our outdoor showerhouse. Even in my worst dreams back home, I had not been able to picture this nerve-tensing setting. Nor had I been able to imagine the scope of destitution and illness that thrived among the poor of all ages in some of the areas where I would work.

I was no stranger to illness, and wherever I saw ailing children in particular I was reminded of my own childhood. I had always been a sickly youngster, plagued with a series of sinus and ear infections, colds and what-not. I also was a skinny, hunched kid. I used to put rocks in my dress pockets on weight-taking day in the public schools of Decatur, Illinois, because I was ashamed of being underweight. In the summer I played baseball, swam, rode a bike and did all the usual things a child does; but the winters seemed to be always something of sitting by the window and looking out at the other kids playing in the snow, or lying in bed waiting for the family doctor to arrive with his horrible-tasting nostrums.

School was a bore. I disliked practically every minute of it, although I managed somehow always to pass to the next grade. When I was six years old, the cutest, most lovable Toy Terrier, Zipper by name, helped pass the classroom time. I would daydream what games we would play after school. Zipper was a compromise in our house. I had a cat, but my big brother Bill was allergic to its hair. When the cat was in the house, Bill would sneeze and cough, and he sometimes sounded as though he were choking.

My parents explained they would find a good home for the cat. In exchange, they would give me an unusual surprise at Christmas. Zipper was the surprise, except that I did become suspicious that a dog was on the way. A few weeks before Christmas, my father took me into his confidence that he was going to build a small magazine rack as a present for my mother, and did I want to help? Every night after dinner, we would go down to the basement and work in secret on the rack. Only it did not seem as though it were for magazines—more like a small bed, maybe for a little dog. One night my curiosity was just too much to contain.

"Is the surprise a puppy dog?"

Pop frowned a little, put down the hammer, slowly drew a cigaret from its pack and lit it. He seemed to be taking an unusually long time to do it. "Dog?" he finally asked. "What are you talking about?"

"You know, Pop. This thing for Mom . . ."

"Shhhhhhh," he shushed. "Not so loud or your mother will hear you. We can't give away our secret now, can we?"

"No," I said. Pop went back to work.

The Saturday before Christmas, when Bill and I walked into the house after a movie downtown, a snowy white ball of fur leaped out of Pop's arms and sprinted to us. The rack was not that at all; it was a bed for this cuddly little thing that never walked but zip-zipped around the house. That is how it got its name, Zipper.

Neighbors credited Zipper with saving a little boy's life a few years later. There was a grade on our street. The child was on the sidewalk riding a tricycle when it began gaining too much momentum for him to stop before coming to a busy traffic intersection. Zipper raced after the boy and caused him to topple from the tricycle. It was one of those rare times when Zipper did not chase automobiles. He loved to do that. And then, one night in my senior year at St. Teresa's Academy in Decatur, Zipper chased his last car. My parents had taken him for his evening's stroll when, all of a sudden, he darted toward an automobile, but at the last split-second could not turn away in time. He died the next day. I cried that night and many nights after that because Zipper was one of the dearest friends I ever had. We were always able to communicate. The piano lessons, for example. They started when I was nine years old. My mother played and thought I should, too, but I hated the piano and put up an awful fuss. That did not help, but Zipper tried. He would hang around the bench, whimper sympathetically, disappear and come back dragging the leash.

"Hey, Mom," I would call out while snapping on the leash, "Zipper has to go out." We would make a beeline for the front door. Outside, he would cock his head, look up and spread his mouth in a funny little grin that seemed to say, "That's usin' the old noodle, kid." We did not hurry back, either. Of course, my mother was not fooled. She started intercepting us at the door to take over the dog-walking detail.

"It's strange," she said one afternoon after being out with Zipper less than five minutes, "how your dog required such lengthy walks with you, but he really doesn't have to take one when I'm along."

I knew then that our little game was over. Still, with all the practice, the piano and I were not compatible; the sounds that came out were awful. Maybe my parents thought I was tone deaf or all thumbs. The lessons did not last much longer, and Zipper and I were free to take long walks again. But we did not. There was not anything urgent to do in the house, such as practicing the piano, that required us to vanish.

Much later on, it came as a shock to my father (mother died when I was twelve years old) that I wound up play-

ing drums in the Knox College concert band. And now
he will find out for the first time the reason why: I liked
a drummer in the school band. I also liked rhythm and
the sound of a good beat in the percussion section, and
still do for that matter.

After the piano lessons went kaput, there came dancing
lessons. My parents were persistent in spoon-feeding their
only daughter with the arts. The dancing lessons turned
out badly, too. One afternoon, while practicing steps in
the bedroom, I slipped on the hardwood floor and struck
a shoulder in the fall. The blow damaged a nerve, and my
left arm and hand were paralyzed for a while. Pop dragged
me around to a lot of doctors' offices and finally to Chicago,
where a specialist prescribed a series of corrective proce-
dures that brought the arm and hand back to full useful-
ness.

By this time, I was eleven years old, and Pop decided,
I suppose, that I was more suited for the outdoor life than
the drawing room and ballroom world. He started taking
me on small-game hunting trips. Although I have no recollection of ever having shot anything, Pop still insists
that I was pretty good with a 20-gauge, double-barrel
shotgun. One thing for certain, it was a lot more fun tramp-
ing over the fields with Pop and the Beagles in the frosty
November air than trying to become a "lady."

Not too many months after that first hunting season, a
church event played a major role in deciding my future.
(Actually, there were two unrelated occasions that happened to come close together.) It was a lecture by Dr.
Hyla S. Watters, a Methodist medical missionary in China
who had been interned and later repatriated by the Japanese during World War II. A few months after her return to the United States at the end of 1943, she spoke at
my family's church, the First Methodist in Decatur. Dr.
Watters told of Chinese boys my age, and younger, and

old men dying in battle for their country. She spoke of the widespread illness and hunger, and mothers and babies succumbing from lack of food and medicines all because major supply lines had been cut off by the Japanese troops. She related instances of families and entire villages walking as much as a thousand miles, sometimes more, to escape the advancing Japanese. She appealed to our parishioners to be prepared to help with money, supplies and manpower, especially in the field of medicine, after China was liberated. I remember distinctly the exact words in that part of her appeal:

"I wonder what young people among you will go out to China after the war."

I almost raised my hand. I was ready, right then and there, to go to China and help. At the reception after her lecture, I told her this would be my life's work. She was a gracious lady, sweet and lovable. She wrote down my address, and a few years later sent a Christmas greeting from China following her return by the way of India and The Hump. The greeting was a woodblock print of a Christmas scene on thin, red paper. Dr. Watters is retired now and living in Tupper Lake, New York. Her name and fame as a humanitarian linger, though, among the Chinese. Many of the sisters of the Our Lady of China community remember her from their days on the China mainland.

The second event that helped mold my future took place a few months after Dr. Watters was in Decatur. It, too, had a China setting, for it was the motion picture adaptation of Pearl S. Buck's *Dragon Seed*. This gripping story of Chinese perseverance in the war with Japan made me want more than ever to go to China and help the Chinese in any way possible. Not only help, but become Chinese among the Chinese. The movie made me cry all the way home. My parents were upset that it had been too adult. It was not that at all. I was simply brokenhearted by the suffering borne by my friends the Chinese. From then on, my reading interests and thoughts were slanted toward China. My dreams centered around the day I would set foot on Chinese soil and start living and working as one of the people.

My brother Bill also gave my dreams a lift, but in an oblique way. He was an LST commander, serving in the South Pacific. My ears were glued to the radio for news of the war. This also meant news from China: the stalwart determination of the Chinese and their leader, Generalissimo Chiang Kai-shek, plus the thrilling stories of American pilots flying The Hump with supplies for beleaguered Chinese. There were other influences to come later on. One was Dr. Tom Dooley, whom I met at Crossroads Students Center in Chicago; Sister Catherine Chang of the Sisters of Our Lady of China studying at Marquette University; and a biography about Father Vincent Lebbe, a Belgian who became Chinese among the Chinese.

While I was still a pre-teen-ager, I decided on a career in medicine. This was influenced, of course, by Dr. Watters' lecture. Still, I was not interested in school, and the grade and junior high school teachers at that time did not seem interested in inspiring the youngsters to study harder. At least I never felt any classroom inspiration. It was not until after a year in boarding school that the academic world began to assume any meaning. My father, who was then tax and real estate manager for the Illinois Power Company, said one night, a few months after my mother's death:

"Gloria, I do not think I am doing a very good job of raising you alone. You need sort of a 'second mother.' Perhaps it would be better that you go away to school . . . some place with mature, understanding women teachers who can help you much better than I in adjusting to all the changes encountered in the early teens."

Pop has always been a thorough and practical man. It

was only typical that he fully investigated many schools before making a decision. The fact that he was an active Methodist had no bearing on his decision to send me to a Catholic school, St. Mary's Academy at Notre Dame, Indiana. So, with Pop driving and the car's trunk loaded with suitcases, Gloria Joan Watts was off to boarding school for her sophomore year. It did not work out well in many ways. The principal reason was the unhappiness away from home. In the Fall, there were thoughts of missing the hunting trips with Pop. And, naturally, there was Zipper and wondering what he was doing. I lasted through the year. One good thing, however, was that my grades climbed from a low C average to a B at St. Mary's. I returned home as a day student at St. Teresa's Academy for my junior and senior years. It was there that I blossomed even more academically. The sisters at St. Mary's and St. Teresa's instilled a desire to learn.

One of these was Mother Paul Ketter, my Latin tutor at St. Teresa's, and one of my best friends. She played a paramount role in shaping my life. She was truly a saint. She was patient, understanding, gentle and even prophetic. During one of the frequent visits with her after school, she listened to the umpteenth time about my dreams of going to China.

"Gloria," she finally said, "I have a feeling that you will become a nun someday."

I was stunned. I was not even a Catholic. So how could I become a nun! Furthermore, Mother Ketter was one of the few nuns I was not in awe of. No, they were not mean or domineering, or anything like that. It was something I never could quite put my finger on, except that their habits were so austere and gave the impression that the wearers had never been children or teen-agers. Naturally, I have since learned differently. Nuns were kids, too, at one time.

"Huh, uh!" I blurted, amazed that she even thought such a thing, let alone say it to me. When I first went to St. Teresa's, I made it perfectly clear to the principal, Mother M. Clotilde, that I did not want to have anything to do with the Catholic religion and would not tolerate being preached at. I was there only to obtain a secular education. All the nuns acceded to my wishes. "You've got it all wrong, Mother. A medical missionary? Yes. A nun? No. I could never be a nun for the simple reason that I will never be a Catholic. You know, of course, that I enjoy religion, but I am perfectly happy in my own church."

A decade later, when I began my novitiate with the Sisters of Our Lady of China, I took Paul as one of the names partly to honor the memory of Mother Paul Ketter. She had died of complications from a broken hip. The fracture took place the day I left for Chicago to work as a lay missionary with Asian students. I had just been graduated from St. John's Hospital School of Nursing in Springfield, Illinois, and we had planned a good-by get-together at the Ursuline Sisters' convent in Decatur. The nuns said Mother Paul Ketter, who then was in her seventies, decided to meet me at the bus stop near the convent. She fell while walking through the garden.

While at St. Teresa's, eight of us, four boys and four girls, palled around together, starting in junior year. In the summer, we went swimming, bike riding and to the movies. I was a true-blue movie fan; every movie had a one-word description, "great." During school months, the eight of us played canasta at my parents' home, went to dances and movies once in a while, but more often met at the neighborhood drugstore and sat in a booth talking, laughing and drinking Cokes. Oddly enough, we never talked about our futures, except once in a while to exchange data about parental "influence" on the choice of a college or university. We were typical teen-agers: parents were to be seen (when we needed money) but not heard. There was something unusual about our group. Four of us eventually entered religious lives, three of the boys and myself. Tom Gallenbach, Andrew Parks and John Sohms became priests. I joined the Our Lady of China community.

For me, college was inevitable. I wanted to become a physician, a medical missionary in China. Pop also was a firm believer in a college education. He highly recommended Knox College in Galesburg, Illinois. There was a sentimental reason. Bill was graduated from Knox. He majored in English preparatory to becoming a newspaperman. Knox also had a pre-med school. And what did Gloria Joan Watts think about Knox? Nix on Knox. I loved my brother with all my heart. He was twelve years older than I, and a sweet, kind, thoughtful person. He was always trying to do something for his kid sister, such as carrying me on his bike while he delivered newspapers, taking me to ball games, and helping me avoid chores around the house. Then, too, he was a war hero who commanded the LST that carried General Douglas MacArthur back to the Philippines. Bill was somebody to look up to and I did. Still, when it came to college, maybe Knox was fine for newspaperman William E. Watts, Jr., but not for future physician Gloria Joan Watts. That was where the line was drawn. I had my own ideas about a pre-med school preference.

So, I went to Knox and became a drummer in the concert band and an excellent bridge player by way of nightly sessions around the card tables at the students' lounge, resulting in a C average from lack of study, and also an avid reader of comparative religion at the college library. At the end of the freshman year, I went back home and broke the news to the family: no more Knox. My medical career was on the rocks. Medical schools frown on C averages offered by candidates for admission. All in all, I had gone through a silly rebellion, although not an un-usual one for many teen-agers. In retrospect, however, somebody in my family should have knocked my head off for having been so mule-stubborn.

All was not lost, though. There were the college credits that were to come in handy later on. And there was com-parative religion. The reason for the keen interest in that subject had its foundation in my senior year at St. Teresa's. Although none of the sisters there even vaguely tried to influence me toward religion, I had found much comfort in going into the school's chapel to pray. Then, one spring day in my senior year, another non-Catholic girl friend had asked me to go along to our church where she had permission to use the piano. While she practiced, I had wandered upstairs into the main part of the church to pray. I was startled by a sudden feeling of its emptiness. There was always His Presence in the chapel at school, but it did not seem the same here for an odd reason that I could not explain. I began to wonder more about religion, par-ticularly about different groups and churches. Did one church have more to offer than another? If so, why? And why did I feel the emptiness in this church but not in the school chapel? As near as I can determine, that day was the religious turning point in my life. I mulled the ques-tions for months before making the decision to become a Catholic. Pop frowned on the idea. I turned to my step-mother, Jo, for support. (My father had remarried when I was fourteen years old.) Jo was a Catholic, but she sided with him. They both agreed that this was probably a spur-of-the-moment, teen-ager's notion. It was not. It was, instead, a conversion from within. I persisted and Pop finally said, all right, we would go to see Monsignor George Powell at St. Patrick's Church, Jo's parish in Decatur.

"You are positive that you want to take this step?" Mon-signor Powell asked.

"Yes. Very much." I was certain that he would arrange immediately for me to begin instruction, maybe even start that night.

He sat silent for a while. "Well, Gloria, I want you to understand that this is not the same thing as buying an ice cream cone, or a new dress." His tone was not at all optimistic. "You are going to have to wait a year. If you still feel the same way, come back and we'll talk about it some more."

I was terribly disappointed. It's easier to break out of jail, I thought, than to get into the Catholic Church. The thought almost tumbled out of my mouth, but, for once, I kept it shut. Then came the year at Knox. I preferred reading books on comparative religion in the library than studying the prescribed college courses. On returning home from Knox, I was determined more than ever to convert. Monsignor Powell kept his promise to see me.

"True," he said after listening to the year's activity, "you have given thought and study to becoming a Catholic. But I believe you should wait a little longer."

I bristled. "I am not going to wait any more. If you won't accept me, I'll find another priest who will." Monsignor Powell must have realized that I was not going to be put off, because he arranged for a priest to begin instruction.

That summer of 1951 was not a thoroughly happy one. Although I had achieved one goal, conversion, there had been failure in another, medicine. Pop and Jo knew how determined I had been about using my hands and knowledge to heal the sick. They suggested another college with a pre-medical school, but I had had enough of college life. Still, I realized that if I ever did go to the Orient—at this point, the dream was badly deflated and I was down in the dumps—I would have to have all the practical knowledge and skill I could get in medicine. This led naturally to a consideration of nursing as a career for me. We began checking out schools, and the choice narrowed to the Franciscan nuns at St. John's Hospital in Springfield. There were two advantages to St. John's. One, it was close to home; and, two, there would be an opportunity to take additional credits in hospital administration and other related subjects. Such courses were made available in off-duty hours by the Franciscan Fathers at nearby Quincy College.

Unlike most of today's student nurses, whose training is more centered around textbook education and less bedside work, our schedule at St. John's was geared more to dealing with the patients directly. We had plenty of classroom work with detailed study of different diseases, to be sure, but we also gave hypodermics, took blood from patients for lab work-ups, spent months in surgery, learned how to give intravenous feedings, how to use a stethoscope, how to take blood pressure readings and other technical medical duties. We also made rounds with the physicians, took notes on patients' illnesses and medical care. After the rounds, the doctors discussed their cases with us. We learned plenty in those discussions. St. John's was an 800-plus-bed hospital at that time, with outlying hospitals for tuberculosis and crippled children. It had patients with just about every disease and ailment in the medical books. There was plenty of opportunity to learn something about medicine, and I began to take full advantage of the opportunities. Instead of going on dates, I would stay in the hospital and read medical books. Naturally, with such a busy schedule, time flew and graduation day in 1954 seemed to arrive before I even unpacked my bags. Pop, Jo, Bill and his wife, Phyl, came over from Decatur for the exercises. They beamed; I beamed; and then Pop jabbed the college needle again.

"Gloria, this lay missionary work in Chicago you have been talking about going into . . ." he paused.

"Yes, Pop, what about it?"

"It sounds fine and all, and we are proud that you want to devote your life to helping other people."

This was a real snow job, and he was not fooling anybody. We all knew what was on his mind, but nobody interrupted.

"Yes," he went on, "that is an unselfish approach to life. But, Gloria, have you thought of this: you might go there, like it—and we all hope you do like it—but you'll stay on and on. Next thing you know it'll be too late for college. Now, if it's a matter of money . . ."

It was better to get this matter settled right then and there. "No, Pop," I interrupted, "it's not a question of money or going back to college. It's a question of doing something I think should be done. You know how I had my heart set on going to the Orient. I just can't get the missionary bug out of my system. But here is a chance to do some missionary work in America among Asian students. That's what I want to do. After a while, if I see that finishing college will help in some way, I'll go back. That's a promise."

There were many missionary opportunities in Chicago. There was Father Jacques and his Vietnamese and Philippine Catholic Action groups that often met at Crossroads Students Center. Crossroads offered a sanctuary—a home away from home—for hundreds of young people from a dozen or so countries in the Far East who were studying at colleges and universities in Chicago and other areas. The Center, operated by the International Catholic Auxiliaries, was staffed with lay people, who, in a real sense, were missionaries. The China spark flamed again, although going to China itself was out of the question because of the Communist take-over of the mainland. But, I reasoned, mainland China was not the only place in the Far East. There was Taiwan, a province of China, to which Chiang

Kai-shek had moved democratic China's government. There were Indonesia, Thailand, Vietnam, Laos and Burma. Maybe, just maybe, something would develop in Chicago. Well, it did in the shape and enthusiasm of Dr. Tom Dooley, the American physician who devoted his life to the people of Vietnam and Thailand. He visited Crossroads shortly after his first return to the United States for a brief visit, and I met him for the first time there.

Tom Dooley's constant appeal was that doctors and nurses must go to the Far East to counteract the Communists. "They are telling people that the Americans are barbarians and will kill and eat them," he said. "We must have more Americans to show the people in Vietnam and the other countries out there threatened by Communism that we are humans and we are humanitarians. It is the simplest and most effective way to make the Communists out as liars. Once they lose face, the people will be more inclined to listen to our side of the story."

I had also heard many stories about Father Vincent Lebbe, founder of International Catholic Action. Father Lebbe was a frail little Belgian priest who had gone out to China and become "Chinese among the Chinese." Many Westerners scoffed at him and even placed innumerable roadblocks in his path. Still, he persisted despite seemingly insurmountable odds and became one of the Catholic Church's finest "ambassadors" to China and, at the same time, a national hero to the Chinese. His was an inspiring story. Between it and Dr. Dooley's enthusiasm, the die was cast. Orient, here I come. Well, not quite that fast.

I believed that I needed more training in public health work. Marquette University in Milwaukee, Wisconsin, was highly recommended, and I went there in the fall of 1956. As it turned out, Marquette had more to offer than a bachelor's degree in public health. Sister Catherine Chang of the Our Lady of China community was a chemistry student there before continuing her studies in X ray. Sister Catherine was one of the fourteen survivors of the community's two-year-long flight to safety from mainland China when the Communists seized control. Her stories of that awful, awful experience and the community's struggles to exist after being re-established in Taiwan never ceased to hold my rapt attention. In a nutshell, I was goggle-eyed. And then came the realization that this is what I had been looking for. Public health would fit in beautifully with the community's work among the people, many of them mountain folk far removed from the benefits of good medicine. I asked Sister Catherine if she thought I would be of any value to the Sisters of Our Lady of China.

"Help? Value? You don't mean . . ." She stopped and her face lit up.

"Yes, I mean."

Sister Catherine bit her lower lip. She quickly turned somber. A frown darkened her features. "Maybe I have done something wrong," she said. "Maybe I have talked too much. Gloria, you have had dreams of going to China, but you are an American girl. You are not used to hardship. Our mother house is in the mountains, not in a big and bustling city with movies, television, air conditioning, bathrooms and all sorts of comforts and conveniences you are used to. Our mother house is made of mud and bamboo. It is nothing like you have been accustomed to. Many times the sisters have to carry water. In the winter, there is no heat. The food is different. Sometimes there is not very much of it."

It all sounded so romantic. Imagine living in a mud and bamboo house and carrying water from the village well. Maybe a bonfire to keep warm on a cold winter's night. Why, it would be like reliving the adventurous wagon-train days in our country's glorious pioneering era. Oh, what strange imaginations American movie and TV horse operas can conjure up in the minds of the innocent.

"I would like to go there," I insisted. Sister Catherine could have talked until she was blue in the face. All I was interested in was whether the community would accept me as a lay missionary. The word finally came back. Yes. It was sent along by the superior general, Mother Philomena Ly. She suggested a two-year stay, if possible. You can bet your life it was possible! Only two things stood in the way: finishing college and finding a job to earn enough money for passage to Taiwan. Pop would have given me the latter, but I did not want to burden him, as he was close to retirement. Because of past college credits and extra work taken at Marquette, graduation came at mid-term in 1959. Then off to Chicago, where there was a job waiting at Michael Reese Hospital. The nine months at Michael Reese turned into a blur, partly because of the excitement about going to Taiwan and partly due to working double shifts to earn money faster. I was in a hurry to reach the Sisters of Our Lady of China.

CHAPTER TWO

The black hull of the *Hai-min* (Ocean Brightness), already satiated with cargo, sat low in the water at its wharf in Seattle. Slings bulging with still more crates and cartons swung gracefully up off the dock, high into the air, then dropped out of sight through the gaping deck wells and down deep into the freighter's hold. Big trucks and little dock carts moved importantly all around me as I stood entranced and rooted to the dock. My heart was going mile-a-minute; here was romance, the busy port, the unknown of the sea, the huge Pacific Ocean beyond. This freighter would be my home for the next twenty days as it plowed through the Pacific and into the East China Sea, finally tying up at Keelung, Taiwan's principal northern port and about fifteen miles from the capital city of Taipei. It was four o'clock in the afternoon when I went up the gangplank. The date was November 8, 1959. I could not forecast then that this would be my last time on American soil until five years later, a time span that would bring tremendous and rich dimensions to my life.

Aboard ship, there was the last-minute bustling before sailing. Most of the passengers—there were twelve of us, mostly Chinese students on their way home to Taiwan— were already aboard. I hit it lucky right away. My cabin mate was a bright-eyed, vivacious, happy young woman.

"Hello," she said as I walked through the doorway. "You

are Gloria Watts, yes? I am Bette Wang." Bette had been
a student in the United States and was eagerly looking
forward to rejoining her family in Taipei. She and her
family (her father was General Y. A. Wang, an army medical doctor and hospital administrator in Taipei) were
among the 2,000,000 mainlanders who had escaped from
the Communists and taken up new homes on China's democratic island of Taiwan.

"Hello, Bette," I said. "But how did you know my name?"

"Oh, very simple. I asked the purser."

From that moment on, we got along famously. I wanted
to learn Chinese, starting right away. Bette obliged. We
had a ball, Bette the teacher and I the student. I found
out quickly that Chinese is not an easy language for the
Westerner. It is a "picture" language as opposed to our
ABCs. Also, as many as eighty different inflections on one
word can create that many different meanings. Moreover,
if a word is dropped from a phrase or a sentence, the
entire meaning can be changed. Thus, the Chinese I learned
aboard ship was negligible, and some of it was even the
classical type of Mandarin that is no longer used on Taiwan. Nevertheless, a few evenings after we had started
the lessons, Bette told everybody as we sat down to dinner
how well I was coming along with the language.

"Go ahead, Gloria; say something," she urged.

Well, this was as appropriate a time as any to let everybody know that I was hungry. I let the words pop out,
"*Wo yao fan.*" There were some eye-raised glances ex-
changed around the table before everybody began smiling. I was pleased no end over having made such a good
impression, and leaned over to thank Bette in English, of
course, for having made my debut such a success.

She had a devilish grin. "Do you know what you said?"

"Why, yes." I was surprised that she should ask. "I said,
'I am hungry.'"

"Huh, uh. 'I am a beggar.'"

I had left out the word *chih—Wo* * *yao chih fan.* The world caved in. I felt like a fool. Bette reacted quickly and graciously. "You should feel good," she said. "Everybody is complimented that you want to learn our language."

Looking back now, it was a prophetic error. I did become a beggar in many ways and many times—for money, medicines and medical supplies to help us, the Our Lady of China community, that is, in furthering our work. The begging is not finished; it will go on for a long time.

It is a strange thing, though, how a little mistake, innocently made, can sometimes cement human relations. From then on, after the "beggar" speech, everybody on board was eager to help with the Chinese lessons. The other passengers also wanted more details about my destination and plans there; and why I, an American, chose a Chinese ship over a United States-flag carrier. The latter was easier to explain than the destination. One thing, the passage was $280 on the *Hai-min* as against $500 on American lines. The $220 difference meant an earlier start to Taiwan. Secondly, if I were going to live Chinese, why not start immediately via a Chinese boat to get to know the Chinese at close quarters, learn something about their culture, try to pick up some of the language, and become accustomed to the food and use of chopsticks. If only the captain, C. Y. Hsu, had cooperated on the food. Captain Hsu made certain that every meal was a Chinese feast, and I gorged myself. I also gained five pounds.

As for the destination, I knew only that it was Chiayi-something. All the correspondence with Mother Philomena Ly had been conducted through Sister Catherine, who had acted as the interpreter. The passengers explained that there were two Chiayis, a city on the main railroad line

* Note: Wo is first person pronoun I. Thus, capping the W.

and about 150 miles south of Taipei; and Chiayi County, of which the city is the county seat. They were concerned how I would ever find the sisters until I finally was able to make them understand that Mother Philomena would be at the dock. Everybody relaxed then and began telling captivating stories about Chiayi, the county.

"Oh," one shipmate cried out, "you will see beautiful *Ali-shan.*" That prompted a songfest, one of many we had on board, to teach me *Ali-shan te ku niang,* (The Maiden from Mt. Ali). This mountain, some 13,000 feet high and the tallest in Taiwan, is one of the island's foremost and most famous scenic spots. It is covered with snow much of the year. Although Mt. Ali is in the northwest corner of Chiayi County, I have never been there. My life in Taiwan has just been too crowded for sight-seeing.

I had a lot of time to think and pray as we crossed the Pacific. In fact, it was the first time in years that there was a chance to sit down and really review and plan my life calmly. I considered three avenues: (1) return home after two years and settle down in public health work, (2) get married, or (3) spend the rest of my life as a lay missionary in the medical field either in Taiwan or elsewhere in the Orient. There were no thoughts of becoming a nun. The three choices became clear; the next two years would determine my future. After all, I was twenty-seven years old; it was about time to think seriously of settling down.

Because of excellent weather, the *Hai-min* made fast time, cutting two days off her schedule. Bette Wang and I planned to use those days in showing me the sights, including a long-dreamed introduction to the Chinese theater. Bette invited me to stay at her house in Taipei, and we would let Mother Philomena know where to find me. Everything went fine until we docked. For one thing, the low-hanging clouds began to sprinkle just after we had opened our suitcases for customs inspection on the *Hai-min*'s open deck. I had eight suitcases and packing boxes, all crammed with clothing, medical textbooks and equipment. By the time we were able to cover the opened gear to protect the contents from the rain, it did not matter much. Luckily, it was a light rain, and they were only dampened. Usually, when it rains in Taiwan, there is no fooling around. It pours.

When we disembarked, Bette's parents and a dozen relatives were on hand to greet her. Her father had brought along a bus. He needed it for that mob. But lo and behold! there was Mother Philomena, two days ahead of time. She had been in daily contact with the steamship lines and learned of the earlier arrival.

Mother could not speak English. I could not speak Chinese. Bette, who could speak both languages, was busy being welcomed by the flock of relatives. And among the Chinese, there is no such thing as hurrying a greeting, such as is done in the United States. "Hi, hello, boy; it's great to be home, and here's a friend I want you to meet; hey, Gloria, my parents," and zip-zip to the next person. The Chinese make it a ceremony, and it is a really warm affair, too.

But there was Mother Philomena chattering away in my direction and in Chinese. Her shoe-button brown eyes glistened happily. Even though I could not understand a word she said, I liked her right away. She gave the impression of being a substantial person—a first impression, by the way, that was correct. She was about five feet, three inches tall, and lean. She was not alone. There was a Chinese priest, Reverend John Pai, the Taipei representative of the Most Reverend Thomas Niu, the bishop of the Chiayi diocese. He did not speak English, either. There was also Sister Edna of the Holy Ghost community, an American nun who had spent years in China but now was working temporarily with the Our Lady of China community. (Sister Edna returned to her own community the following summer on reassignment.)

And then out of nowhere appeared a middle-aged man.

I remembered him as one of the passengers. Aboard ship, he had been quiet and reserved. Some of the passengers said he was a businessman from Taipei. He spoke to Father Pai and Mother Philomena before turning to me. "I talk English; I help," he said. I was surprised, as I had not heard him speak anything but Chinese during the crossing. I looked questioningly at Sister Edna. Mother Philomena had brought her along to do the interpreting. Sister Edna gave a slight shrug, indicating it was protocol to defer to the volunteer interpreter. The Chinese have rigid rules about courtesy. It would have been impolite of Sister Edna to explain to him that she was an American, fluent in Chinese, too, and could handle the translation. He would have lost face. So, he took over.

I carefully explained my plans to stay with Bette Wang in Taipei for two days because of the freighter's early arrival. He nodded and nodded. "Finish?" he asked. He turned to Mother Philomena and began rattling off Chinese a mile a minute. Out of the corner of my eye it seemed that Sister Edna's face had turned quizzical, but I was more intent on watching Mother Philomena's reaction. The Chinese rarely show emotion, but suddenly there were tears in her eyes. I was nearly overwhelmed by this seemingly warm reception, and concluded that she was showing happiness. As soon as she started speaking, my conclusion began to waver. There was an undercurrent of sharpness that did not need translation.

The volunteer turned to me, a frown on his face and some belligerence in his voice. "Mother Ly has a specially nice room for you. Don't you want to go?"

That did not make any sense. Fortunately, Bette Wang and her family finished their greetings about this time, and Bette hurried over to our group to invite everybody to go along in the bus. "We'll drop off the priest and sisters wherever they want to go, and you'll come along with us," she told me. Bette thought everything had been arranged for my two-day visit.

"Wait a minute, Bette," I said. "Something seems to be all mixed up here. Maybe you can straighten it out." I quickly filled her in on what I had tried to get through to Mother Philomena about our plans. Bette spoke to her for a few minutes, and Mother Philomena replied at length.

Bette looked back at me. It was obvious that something displeased her, too. "Have you changed your mind?" she asked, abruptly.

"Changed what mind about what?" I was even further in the dark about this strange turn in the conversation.

"You know . . . what you told this man here. That you are not going with the sisters after all; that you are going to Taipei and look for medical work there. You never said anything like that on the boat."

I was flabbergasted and reassured Bette that there had been no change in plans other than to spend the two days with her.

"All right," she said, "I'll explain that again, but I do not think she's going to believe me. She thinks I influenced you to live in Taipei." Bette went back to Chinese and talked to Mother Philomena fully four minutes. Mother's eyes began widening a little, her head started to move up and down, and her lips pursed into an "oh" before she answered.

"The whole thing's a mess," Bette finally told me. "She thought you were chickening out. By the way, how did *he*, the little Helpful Henry, come into the picture? We rarely ever heard a word out of him on the boat. Anyhow, he doesn't speak English. He just speaks at it."

That was my first experience with "speaking at" a language. There would be more. Now that I look back on them, they are good for a lot of nostalgic laughs. At the time they were going on, though, they were far from funny.

Standing and gabbing there on the dock, we finally

arrived at a compromise. Mother Philomena had planned to take an early afternoon train back to the convent as she had a mountain of work waiting. She agreed, however, to stay on until that night in order to let me spend a little time with Bette and her family. Things were finally worked out to take the nine o'clock train. Later, after I had learned the language, Mother Philomena and I did a lot of amusing reminiscing about that day on the dock in Keelung. She also said that when she arrived at the Wangs to take me in tow, she had doubts that I would stay out the week.

The Wangs made me feel right at home. On the boat, Bette had explained that it would be proper manners for me to address her family as adopted father, adopted mother and adopted brother. She taught me the words. When I said *kan pa-pa* to the father, and so on through the family, the Wangs adopted me. The Westerner who earnestly tries to adapt himself to the Orient, such as using chopsticks and learning the language and customs, wins favor. All through the dinner, the family took turns complimenting me, but never directly. That would have been bad manners. Rather, one would turn to another and say, for example, "Doesn't she use her chopsticks well!" or, "Our adopted *Mei-kuo-nü-er* (American) daughter is truly Chinese."

The compliments were wonderful, but the dinner was a super challenge. The Wangs had a sixteen-course dinner and used the long, festive-type chopsticks. The length of the chopsticks is governed by the number of courses and people. If it is a small gathering and only a few dishes are on the table, shorter chopsticks are used. If it is a large affair, the longer ones come into play, the reason being that the bowls and platters of food are, naturally, at a distance from the diner and he is going to need all the length possible to reach them. The ones the Wangs used at this feast were much longer than those on the boat. Naturally, they felt clumsy, and even more so for still another reason: they were ivory and, of course, slippery. I had always been used to the bamboo chopsticks. Also, I am left-handed and that complicated matters more. The person to my left was right-handed. Each time we would reach for food, and always in the opposite direction, it seemed, our chopsticks would clash in mid-air with a clackety-clack-clack. It was like a sword duel that I always lost, with the food dropping back onto the platter.

All the while there was chattering, accompanied by side glances at me, and Bette would translate with a straight face. "When you banged that piece of lobster out of Uncle's grasp, your adopted father said, 'Our adopted daughter uses her chopsticks with great dexterity.'" I blushed a deep crimson, which prompted more side glances and chatter. Bette translated, "Your adopted mother said that her adopted daughter has the cheeks of a round, ripe apple."

It so happens that my cheeks are round, and maybe they did look like a "round, ripe apple." By that time, though, I wanted this dinner to be over with in a hurry. But here again, the Chinese are unlike Americans. A feast is something to be savored, to be talked through, and never to be rushed along. I thought we would never get finished. The troubles with the chopsticks were not the only embarrassing thing. The Wangs lived in a Japanese-type house with matting on the floor. Although they used Western furniture, they took their shoes off at the door, in the Japanese manner, and put on slippers. The Chinese feet are much smaller and daintier than Americans', and that meant the slippers covered only the front part of mine. As it turned out, all the walking we had done during the day had worn a big hole in the heel of my stockings. I was positive that everybody had seen it and that it was part of the table conversation. Now that I have been among the Chinese for many years, I am certain that those fears were groundless, as the Chinese do not hold up another's attire or misfortune to ridicule.

With the help of the Wangs, Mother Philomena managed to get me and my pile of luggage to the station on time for the nine o'clock train. Sister Edna said we would go as far as Touliu, a five-hour ride, and stay at a convent overnight.

All of a sudden I was dead tired. It had been a long and exceptionally busy day. Also one filled with emotion. Here I was, finally, in Taiwan and among the Chinese. Years of dreaming, planning, hoping, and even frustrations had jelled into reality. I tried to take a nap on the train, but was much too keyed up to do more than doze fitfully. We took a pedicab from the depot on our arrival at two o'clock in the morning and went directly to the convent adjacent to the Holy Rosary Church. I remember during the pedicab ride that I thought, now I know I am really here, as it was the first time I had ridden in something traditionally Chinese.

The convent was small; it was built of mud and bamboo. It was also where the black, furry spider glowered, and the mosquitoes swarmed. The wood floor also was a problem. It had been honeycombed by either red ants or a form of termites. The spikes on my high-heel shoes sank right into the wood. On top of that, when I moved the sliding closet door to hang up my clothes, it fell out and banged my head. I did not know what to expect next, and decided to keep on the light, a naked bulb hanging from the ceiling, as I was scared half to death. I also was so tired that I ached. Additionally, the contrast between the Wangs' beautiful home in Taipei and this down-country convent building was so great that I wanted to cry. Instead of tears, I tried hard to be practical. Had I made a mistake? It certainly seemed so. Moreover, despite the lessons on the boat, the language seemed insurmountable. Not just one but two. There was Mandarin, the official language. There was Taiwanese, the island dialect that was still the sole tongue of many people in the area served by the Our Lady of China community. Also, instead of a body-molding mattress and soft, billowy, Western-style pillows, this bed—and it was typically Chinese—was a hard straw pallet and the rice-skin pillow like a rock. The wildlife visible on the ceiling and swarming in the air, and also the invisible but surely lurking someplace and ready to slither toward me—well, it was not like anything back home. I toyed with ways of bowing gracefully out of the agreement with the sisters. And then turned right around and railed at myself for being so weak in spirit.

My mind dwelled on the two genteel European women who went out to China and joined Father Lebbe's community as Sisters Luke and Chow, and how they bore up under greater hardships, the least of which was using bricks for pillows. They were nuns and I was a lay missionary, but did that make them stronger than I? The matins bell at six o'clock in the morning was almost a welcome relief from the torturous mental gymnastics. I arose, still aching-tired, dressed and hurried to meet Mother Philomena and Sister Edna and go to mass. I prayed hard for strength.

After mass there was breakfast. I was a guest and that meant there had to be more than *hsi-fan,* a gummy and bland rice porridge that is the mainstay of the Chinese breakfast. (No matter how poor a family is, it always serves a guest a sumptuous breakfast. To do less would mean loss of face.) The sisters went to great pains to prepare a feast for my first breakfast in Taiwan. There was *hsi-fan,* of course, but there were also eggs, vegetables, chicken, pork, pickled watermelon rind, and many, many other things I have since forgotten. I was to learn later that this was a far cry from the usual breakfast of *hsi-fan* that the Our Lady of China sisters had day in and day out. I looked at all this delicious food and wondered how I could save face for myself. I was much too excited—and also tired—to eat with any appetite.

We went to see Bishop Niu after breakfast. He was lean and gentle. His face and hands were delicate, exactly like those in the drawings and paintings of the classical Chinese scholars. Bishop Niu spoke some English and greeted me in my language. Most of the conversation, though, was in Chinese and translated.

"You have come a long way to be with our sisters," he said. "My prayers are with you that your work and the days you spend here with us will be fruitful and that they will bring you great joy."

Bishop Niu arranged for transportation from Touliu, which is on the lush, undulating plains of West-Central Taiwan, to the mother house in a place called Mei-shan, in the rugged, towering mountains that run the entire length of this 230-mile-long island paradise. Mei-shan, which means Plum Mountain, was ten miles south of Touliu, as the crow flies. By ground transportation, it was closer to twenty miles over the then meandering, hair-pin roads leading into the mountains. The transportation was the bishop's jeep. The driver was a bright-eyed, pleasant young man. He helped pile all my eight suitcases and packing boxes sky high on the back of the vehicle. We were off to Plum Mountain. It was such a romantic-sounding name that I could hardly wait to see the place. Moreover, it was such a bright, warm day (Touliu is only about fifteen miles north of the Tropic of Cancer) that the weather and my excitement helped me forget the fatigue. I wanted to get started in the worst way.

To the newly arrived American, traffic in Taiwan appears to be on a first-come, first-served basis. The major difficulty is in determining who came first, you or him. The ensuing middle-of-the-street debate between the accident participants creates a monumental traffic jam, solely because the debaters are oblivious to everything but their own immediate problems. I first noticed the unusual, gang-way, here-I-come traffic pattern from General Wang's bus during the ride from Keelung to Taipei. There were cars, trucks, motorcycles, water-buffalo carts and scads and scads of bicycles, plus heavy foot traffic. There was constant horn honking by the car and truck drivers, beeping by the motorcyclists and bell ringing by the bicyclists in addition to some truly expert broken-field driving and fantastic feats of balancing. Even so, it puzzled me that there were no accidents every few feet, especially crack-ups involving the bicycle freighters. Baskets piled high fore and aft interfered with the cyclists' vision. Yet, they managed somehow to dodge and weave quite nonchalantly through the thick traffic stream. It was no wonder, I thought, that most juggling and balancing acts back in the States had such names as Chang, Wang and Wu. They served their theater apprenticeships on bikes back home.

If I thought traffic was on the wild side, by American standards, in the metropolises of the north, I was in for a real treat down here in the farming country that spreads in all directions from Touliu. Ducks, chickens, geese and pigs joined the flow. And lots and lots of human foot traffic, too. The roads were crammed. As in the cities, everybody on wheels figured he had the right of way; everybody on foot assumed the same rigid, unyielding attitude. It was like playing a traffic version of Russian roulette. To help make the game more interesting, the roads were narrow; they were mostly dirt; they twisted and turned around blind curves as they headed into the mountains; and, in many instances, they offered such additional obstacles as holes right in the middle of the roadbed.

In the eyes of the average American driver, the Chinese are the kings of the hot-rodders. Our jeep driver was the king of kings. His basic system of free-wheeling was quite elementary: hand on the horn and foot on the gas pedal. Ducks, chickens, everything and everybody scattered, and more often than not just in the nick of time as he cowboyed along. He left behind great, billowing clouds of dust and cackling, honking, squealing fowl and animals. But the lad would not be deterred.

I was scared almost witless. No, worse than that. I was paralyzed from fear. Additionally, every bone and muscle in my body was screaming from pain, for we bounced and bounced and bounced. The seat was a wooden board with a thin, plastic covering. No cushioning at all. I felt like a yo-yo that had been bouncing off a concrete sidewalk for hours on end. Mother Philomena, though, seemed impervious. Maybe she had ridden with this young man before. She never once changed her placid facial expression. The only comment she ever made was a few times in Chinese, followed by a skidding, growling halt. The reason for the stops was that she wanted to introduce me to the Our Lady of China Sisters at three mission stations on the way to Mei-shan. The stops were a welcome respite, but getting back into the jeep was a nightmare of what-next.

We finally roared to a last, dust-blinding stop at the mother house in Mei-shan at four o'clock in the afternoon. Everything was a blur. I was nauseated, headachy, sweaty, dusty and blind-tired. But the day was far from over. There were greetings and introductions to go through. A half dozen sisters were standing in front of the compound gate, waiting for us. They smiled shyly and proceeded to set off a huge string of firecrackers. This was traditional, as it was the Chinese way of saying, welcome, friend, we are overjoyed that you are in our midst.

One of the nuns stepped forward and bent her head in greeting. "Hello, Miss Watts." I was startled for a moment. She spoke English. Or was it something that she had rehearsed? And then there was a sudden recollection of something Sister Catherine had noted back at Marquette, that one of the sisters spoke a little English.

"I am Sister Raphael Chan." The voice was soft, plaintive. Certainly! This was the name Sister Catherine had mentioned, Sister Raphael Chan, the local superior of this Our Lady of China convent.

A fast-gathering crowd of villagers stopped to stare at me in poker-faced silence. Their deep brown eyes were just visible under the brims of the straw, conical hats. Poverty and sickness showed in some of their faces and bodies. They said nothing. They did not wave. They simply stared. Staring is not considered impolite in Chinese custom. If they see something or somebody different from the usual everyday goings-on, they gather around to get a better look. They mean nothing by it; they are simply curious. I was a curio, a *ch'ang-pi-tzu*, a long nose, which is what the Chinese call the Westerners. Of course, it is nicer than what they used to call them, *yang kuei tzu*, foreign devils.

After a while, I was escorted through the wooden gate in the high brick wall that formed the compound. Straight ahead there was a long, low-slung building. It looked like an army barracks, excepting that it was made of mud and bamboo and had a peaked, gray tile roof. On each side of the compound, there were two similar buildings, also made of mud and bamboo. The three structures formed a blocked-U shape. Sister Catherine (she was still studying in the States, by the way) had told me that housing was mud and bamboo in the rural areas of Taiwan. But in my enthusiasm to go there, I had looked on it in a romantic sense. So this was Mei-shan, Plum Mountain. It surely was not Park Avenue.

I was given the VIP room, located at one end of the mother house. It was a small room, no more than ten feet square. There was a wooden bed with a straw pallet, a rice-skin pillow, and the inevitable mosquito netting. There was a straight-back chair, a small table, and a portable clothes closet that was too short to hang dresses in without the hems folding over on the floor. The closet was all right for the Chinese, but I am five feet, six inches tall, a height very few Chinese women attain. Ever after that, whenever I would put on a dress from the closet, the bottom sort of bent to the right or left and I had a feeling that I was walking sideways. Also in the room was a wooden stand with an enamel basin that served as the wash bowl, and an enamel water pitcher.

The low ceiling was cardboard that had been freshly whitewashed. The floor was of a very sandy cement. Huge damp spots showed through, as though it had just been scrubbed. Although the room and everything in it was spotless, the moisture on the floor was a natural phenomenon. This was an exceptionally damp climate, muggy-clammy in the boiling summer and bone-chilling in the winter, even though the temperature never fell to freezing. So there were always patches of dampness on the sandy-cement floor. This, of course, led to arthritis, one of the few chronic ailments I was to pick up.

There was no bathroom in any of the three buildings. What served as one was divided into two separate and distinct outdoor units. One, the toilet facilities, was of the Chick Sales' privy variety. The other was a showerhouse, but not really a shower. Front-line soldiers who had to take a bath out of a helmet will get the idea; only we had buckets and basins instead of helmets.

I had not expected the furnishings and facilities to be comparable to those at the Waldorf. They were not. But I did get room service. Just as I finished jamming the portable closet full of dresses and was trying to figure out where to store the rest of the things from the still untouched mountain of luggage and packing boxes, a knock came on the screen door that led directly from the com-

pound yard into the room. (This was the only door to my
room. In fact, there was no hallway in any of the buildings; all rooms were entered from the yard.) A sister stood
outside the door. She carried a dinner tray, but I was not
hungry. I put the tray on the small table and stared list-
lessly at the food. There was a bowl of rice, a bowl of green
vegetables that did not look familiar, a bowl of boiled pork,
a small cup and pot of tea—and chopsticks. It had been
hours since lunch; I should eat something. In fact, I had
to eat if for no other reason than that it would have been
a serious breach of etiquette to return the dinner. The entire
Our Lady of China community would have lost face, from
Mother Philomena on down to the cook.

Pop and my stepmother, Jo, had written two letters that
were waiting for me. I decided that concentrating on the
letters and mechanically eating at the same time would get
me through most of the food. The Chinese custom of leaving a little of everything in the bowls took on a new and
face-saving meaning, at least for me, as I would have been
unable to finish all the food. The reading-eating plan
worked. Although the letters were newsy, it was not difficult to read between the lines that Pop and Jo were
anxious. They had not been overjoyed by my decision to go
to Taiwan, although living and being Chinese had been
a topic of discussion around the house for many years.
Maybe they thought that as time dragged on the dream
would erode. But now I had to assure and reassure them
that it had been the right decision, that I was happy in
Taiwan, and that the Our Lady of China mother house
was comfortable and modern, even down to a dandy bathroom. True, I wrote a few white lies that night. Still, it
was absolutely necessary to avoid anything that might upset them. Also, in looking back on it now, maybe I did not
want to lose face, either.

Sisters Philomena Ly and Raphael Chan came by to find

out if everything was all right. We talked for a while, with Sister Raphael acting as the interpreter. Finally, Mother Philomena said, "It is getting late; you should go to bed." It was nine o'clock.

Tired as I was, another night on a *tatami*, a straw pallet, did not sound like a beautyrest sleep. There were some mosquitoes buzzing around (they had already started feasting), and my thoughts turned to the question, will there be any huge, black spiders here at Mei-shan?

"All of us go to bed now," Mother Philomena said, interrupting my thoughts. "We get up at 4:45 o'clock in the morning."

My heart sank. A quarter to five in the morning! Back home, that was the milkman's shift. That usually was the time I was turning over for a few more hours of sleep. Whereupon I was given a break; well, part of one.

"You will not have to get up that early," Mother Philomena said. "Mass is not until six o'clock." The two nuns smiled, bowed and left me.

That night, before falling into a deep and exhausted sleep, I prayed more fervently than ever before. It was not the getting up so early that bothered me. I would get used to that. It was the sickness and poverty compared to my plush American life. Those two things had been obvious from Touliu to Mei-shan. Little children with bellies distended, obviously from worms. Other children too thin for their frames, obviously undernourished and probably affected by chronic diarrhea. Women, old before their time, bare-footed and babies strapped to their backs while they worked in the rice paddies and sugar cane fields. Men with bodies permanently bent and their faces worn and pasty from improper diets and long, long hours of back-breaking work. Houses in the mountains that were hardly shacks compared to American standards. These were the people I was to work with, the homes I would visit.

I do not mean to imply that all of Taiwan was like that. It was, and continues to be, a flourishing country. But when I arrived there in 1959, the island was struggling mightily to emerge from a terrible flood that had caused widespread destruction, especially in the lush farming areas that form a major part of Taiwan's economy. It was also trying to recoup from the debilitation caused by World War II. It was incorporating 2,000,000 refugees from the mainland into its native population of about 8,000,000; and it was building a strong, efficient and vigorous army that would repel any attempts by the mainland Communists to destroy their last remaining outpost of democratic freedom. Any one of those four things was in itself a crushing burden that would have destroyed the morale of people with less fortitude. Taiwan, though, was saddled with all four problems. It met them head-on. The fact that the government was able to cut itself free of United States assistance in 1965 was a brilliant testimonial to the determined ambition of the people and their elected leaders.

In the field of medicine there can be no empathy with a patient. I knew that the people like the ones I saw between Touliu and Mei-shan would become my patients. Did I have the fiber tough enough not to let my emotions break me down and thereby hamper what talent I had in treating them with steady hands and in a practical and professional way? Would I fail when a patient needed an antibiotic, and, with the needle poised in mid-air, look at the thin body and say, "How can I add even a tiny bit more to the suffering of this poor soul by a jabbing prick of this needle?"

I prayed earnestly for strength to let me carry on what I had set out to do—lay missionary work in the field of medicine. There was much to be done, but I needed His help to give me the courage to stay on.

And then there was the Our Lady of China community itself. The mud and bamboo buildings were in disrepair.

And the austere furnishings. I was not so naïve as to expect a palace. I was aware, too, that the religious do not want plush comfort in their residences. Adequately furnished? Yes, in conformity with their vows of poverty. But this community was threadbare; it was barely existing. Such knowledge did not come from the surroundings alone. It came, too, from statistics. In five years—dating from the time the sisters had re-established themselves here in the mountains of West-Central Taiwan—only seven had been added to the ranks of the survivors of the flight from the Communists on the mainland of China. That was a pathetically small number, a growth of slightly more than one a year. A major reason for this near-stagnation was that the sisters had no Western support. They were Chinese-founded, Chinese-operated and strictly autonomous. They were not attached in any way at all to any of the large, strong European- and American-based orders from which to draw funds, manpower and strength. They were on their own. Their bishop, the Most Reverend Thomas Niu, helped all he could, but he, too, had limited finances. The Our Lady of China community was only one group he had to care for in a diocese that had only a bare handful of Catholics—or any other Christians, for that matter—to lend their assistance. The principle religion of the land was Buddhism.

In retrospect, it is amazing in a way that there was even a little growth by the community. Other groups of nuns with Western support had ever so much more to offer in vocations (and superior living quarters), such as nursing, hospital administration, social service work, teaching careers, and so forth. The Sisters of Our Lady of China had nothing so grandiose to offer aspirants. Some kindergarten work, some catechistical and medical work, and long hours at farming to provide some food for the table. Those were about all in the way of careers. Was it any wonder, then, that potential candidates went elsewhere?

Also in looking back on those days, I can say this: Mother Philomena and all the sisters were made of iron wills, devotion to humanity, and a deep-seated dedication to God and His work. In my prayers that first night at Mei-shan, I asked for a little of that strength and devotion, and the will-power to stay on for at least six months before making a decision whether to serve out the promised two years in lay missionary work. I am humbly grateful today that God guided me in making that compact with myself. Through Him, I found a rich, new life.

CHAPTER THREE

My first weeks at Mei-shan were jam-packed with new experiences and activity. There were strange sounds, for example, and the lack of those I had been used to back home. There were no screaming sirens and clanging bells from fire engines and ambulances at all hours of the day and night. There were no huge trucks rumbling by every few minutes, gears clashing or air brakes hissing as the drivers changed speed at traffic lights. There were, for that matter, no traffic lights in Mei-shan; it was an off-the-beaten-track town of 25,000 mountain people. There were very, very few automobiles, but some noisy scooters and motorcycles and swarms of bicycles. And rarely did we hear a plane overhead. All the usual noises city dwellers become used to in the States simply did not exist at Mei-shan.

There were other sounds, but they were foreign to my ears. At night, when everything was deathly still except for the buzzing of the ever-present mosquitoes, the wind sometimes would come up and race through the bamboo trees. The rustling was musical, like a lulling, soft whistling. In the daytime, this whistling acted as an obbligato to other sounds: the rhythmic, musical tones of the click-clock, click-clock from the wooden-platformed shoes worn by some of the villagers, plus the calls of the vendors, as they roamed the town. The men's shoes would make deep, hollow almost-bass sounds; the women's were in the alto range; the children's in a high register. When an entire family would come click-clocking along it sounded much like a xylophone, the vendors had different calls peculiar to their trades. For instance, the pig's ear clipper—he nipped an ear to show that a tax had been paid on the animal—played a flute. The man who bought old rags and papers whirred something that sounded like a ratchet, similar to the burring noises at New Year's Eve celebrations in the States.

And there were the constant smoke aromas. I first noticed these in Taipei, where many of the trains and factories use soft coal. The odor was much like that around South Chicago and nearby Gary, Indiana, and other great steel-making centers in the United States. In the smaller cities and the rural and mountain sections, the aroma was from wood and charcoal, the principal cooking fuels in many homes.

The town of Mei-shan itself was a strange sight to a Westerner's eyes. It lay in a high valley, flanked by sharp-rising mountains that had flat, staggered tops, like steps silhouetted against the sky, rather than conical peaks. The town's main street was paved, but most of the side streets were dirt. Gutters were open and served as drainage ditches. The aromas coming up from the gutters were not always pleasant. When the monsoons came the streets were gumbo and there was no demarcation by the gutters; everything simply flowed together. Most of the houses were of mud and bamboo construction; some of the houses and most of the stores had open fronts. Some had peaked, cement-tile roofs of red or gray. Others had thatched roofs and indicated the inhabitants could not afford tile. Some of the houses had only one room. Others had two, or three, and sometimes more rooms. The sizes of the houses were another indication of the economic status of the owners. There were no yards with lawns and huge old maples, or oaks, or elms. Land was much too valuable for such luxuries, even among the more affluent. The soil was put to the practical use of a vegetable garden, some chickens, ducks and geese running around, and here and there a pig sty.

For the most part, the people were farmers or bamboo cutters, and the businesses in Mei-shan were oriented to those industries. There was only one Christian church, the Our Lady of China Church, which stood about a dozen feet beyond the wall that formed the compound of the mother house.

The overall monotony of the buildings actually had no immediate dampening effect on me. Instead, I was able to see something romantic in this. The reason undoubtedly was because this was, in a sense, mainland China, although the people in this particular area were Taiwanese from generations back and few had ever been to the mainland, only 100 miles away across the Straits of Taiwan, to see the homes of their ancestors. Some of the latter came to Taiwan as early as 600 A.D., during the Sui Dynasty, when the island was inhabited by tribes of aborigines whose origin remains a mystery. By the 1500's—300 years after Taiwan had become a protectorate—there were several waves of migration. When the Dutch took control of the southern part of Taiwan in the 1620's, the Chinese population on the island was estimated at anywhere between 100,000 and 200,000. An Amoy warrior, Cheng Cheng-kung (Koxinga) opened a new wave of migration in 1641 when he sailed an army of 25,000 to liberate Taiwan from the Dutch. After the Communist take-over on the mainland in the late 1940's, upwards of 2,000,000 Chinese fled to the island.

Mother Philomena took me on a quick tour of Mei-shan my first morning there. I wanted to mail a log letter. (I had written a daily account of happenings aboard the freighter and finished it with my arrival at Mei-shan.) She also wanted me to meet Father Stanislaus Sun, our parish priest at the Our Lady of China Church. The trip from the mother house to the post office and back to the rectory was made in silence. We could not communicate orally, only in sign language. I reacted to the lovely wild flowers—such as a form of brown-eyed Susan as much as ten feet tall and with a head nearly a foot across, and giant-size, deep red poinsettias—by tugging at the sleeves of her habit, pointing and making happy facial expressions. She would smile and nod in return. Villagers stopped to stare. Children, more bold than the grownups, tagged along in growing numbers. I sort of had the feeling of being the Pied Piper of Mei-shan. They chattered away, and once in a while Mother Philomena turned and rattled off something in Chinese. I tried to read the expressions on their faces for some hint of what was going on. No luck, for here were the inscrutable Chinese.

At the post office, she motioned for the letter in my hand, and turned it over to the postmaster. Back at the rectory, Father Sun was waiting for us. He was of medium build and courtly of manner. I had wondered how we would communicate. My concern was short-lived because he spoke English, although haltingly.

"We have been awaiting your arrival," he said pleasantly. He motioned for both of us to sit down. The chairs were wicker with straight backs. "You know much about medicine, I am told."

"I hope that I will be able to do some good," I replied.

"You will. We are positive of that. There are many who are sick in our parish. They need the skilled hands and knowledge of Western medicine. You see, we are not so fortunate as the people in the North—at Taipei, for example, where there are excellent doctors and good hospitals." He hesitated and nodded his head thoughtfully. "But you are with us now. When do you plan to start treating the sick?"

At the moment, the question was academic and unanswerable in any precise terms. I was still so tired from the trip—more so that even before—that I could not think properly. Furthermore, Mother Philomena and I had not yet had an opportunity to talk about the subject. In fact, I had not seen the inside of the community's clinic. I did that afternoon. It was a small, mud and bamboo building, no larger than nine-by-nine feet, and built against the outside wall of the convent's compound.

The few bottles of medicine in a small, glass case were as inadequate, to a Westerner's eyes, as the physical dimensions of the dispensary itself. There were some vitamins, aspirins, dysentery medicine and a bare handful of antibiotics. To be truthful, I had seen crossroads, back-country grocery stores in the United States with better-stocked shelves. There were a pair of surgical scissors and a short-blade, hooked knife for lancing boils. The instrument sterilizer was a pot of boiling water on a brick stove in the convent kitchen a block away. There was still another and more serious inconvenience that I was to learn about later: the muggy weather melted the gelatin-coated vitamin and antibiotic capsules. Hundreds upon hundreds were ruined. They needed refrigeration in this climate. We had none for the simple reason that it cost money and the Our Lady of China community was penniless.

This was no clinic as I knew one should be. In hospitals back home, clinics have large waiting rooms with benches and chairs, and the treatment room is large enough for at least a half dozen persons to move about comfortably. The gleaming, white rows of medicine cabinets are well-stocked with everything a doctor-nurse team needs for any sort of an emergency. Other cabinets have dozens of glistening steel instruments for every purpose. There are ample packs of sterile gauze bandages, and containers filled with cotton swabs. No clinic is without at least one instrument sterilizer and a treatment table. When supplies run low, a requisition brings refills in a few hours from the central drug supply room, or, if necessary, in a matter of minutes.

The tiny, mud and bamboo clinic at Mei-shan had nothing even remotely resembling such a dispensary. I felt as helpless as Old Mother Hubbard. I closed my eyes momentarily and said a short prayer, asking for more strengthening of moral fiber and an inkling of where I could put my hands on a large variety of medications, and quickly, too. I was not at all sure what ailments and diseases would walk through the low, narrow door. But whatever they were, they would find the cupboard pretty bare.

I really did not know what sort of a clinic I expected to find. But surely not anything so makeshift and ill-equipped. My spirits dropped with each passing minute spent in the place. I decided that a hot shower or tub bath, whichever was available, would provide an emotional boost. Furthermore, I had not had the refreshing pleasure of a shower since right before getting off the boat the previous morning at Keelung. In between then and that precise moment, my life had been one big hurry-up rush, burdened with major psychological readjustments to the surroundings and such devastating fatigue that I had not had the strength to turn on any spigots or inquire where they were.

Spigots? Mei-shan did not offer such plush living. There was only one and it was outside in the yard. If you saw *South Pacific* and thought its outdoor shower—the roofless cubicle with an overhead tank—was primitive, that shower was twentieth century push-button plumbing when measured against ours. Bathing at Mei-shan was a project. There was no bathtub, only an outdoor showerhouse. We called it that and groaned all the way to the brick stove in the kitchen. The stove was the first step in leading to the "shower." The water, when it was available, was heated in a huge, iron kettle. The fuel was rice skins. They were both cheap and plentiful, as Chiayi was a major part of

Taiwan's rice basket. When the water started to boil, it was ladled into a couple of buckets and carried to the showerhouse, an unheated, five-by-nine-foot, mud and bamboo affair about a hundred feet away. Near the showerhouse was a tap—the spigot—that provided cold water to mix with the hot for the right temperature. And here was still another frustration. Because of a perennial water shortage at Mei-shan, the tap rarely supplied water. A bucket of cold water had to be dipped from a huge, clay storage vat in the kitchen and carried to the showerhouse.

Only then were we prepared to step into the showerhouse, pray that there were no snakes (they would be looking for a dinner of frogs that frequented the small building), and begin the "shower" like this: dip a basin of water from the bucket, pour it over the head, soap up (sometimes I forgot the soap and had to go back for it), rinse off, and continue the process until the "shower" was finished.

When I arrived at the end of November, 1959, the dry season was on. Water was rationed. The village reservoir was on top of the mountain, and the attendant was supposed to turn on the pipeline for an hour or two a day. In the dry season that never happened. This meant, naturally, that water had to be carried from the town well about a half mile from the convent. The sisters and I would form a bucket brigade. Each of us toted two wooden buckets, one on each end of a bamboo pole and slung across our neck and shoulders. The way to the well was downhill, but, naturally, uphill on the return trip with the water-filled buckets. After carrying those heavy buckets sloshing with water for a couple of hours, I got the distinct feeling that water was actually liquid platinum. It was not to be wasted on a daily shower no matter how badly anybody wanted one. The water had a priority rating: cooking, drinking and washing clothes. How much could be stored in the vat? Enough for the absolute essentials. A shower was expendable.

And then there was the damp, winter weather that stretched from December into mid-February. Mei-shan was like a wind tunnel, and the gales sweeping along the valley would burst through the holes under the eaves of the showerhouse and knife right into the marrow. There was an odd human reaction to the cold. The sisters, who had lived in this sub-tropical climate for some years, never seemed to mind the chill. On the other hand, I was from the sub-zero winters of Illinois and Wisconsin. Still, I was the one who nearly froze to death. I used to pray for the luxury of a real shower, with temperature-control spigots and a steam-heated bathroom, while hopping from foot to foot and toweling vigorously in an effort to generate extra body heat. I remember tears of frustration would well up sometimes. They were among the few times I ever cried in my life.

The problems of taking a shower and the fear of snakes were not the only sore spots. There were also vicious little red ants, much like the ones that plague people in some parts of Florida. They bit like crazy, and they were wild for food. Leave a few scraps on the table after a meal and within minutes, it seemed, there would be lines of red ants charging *en masse*. The sisters did everything to combat them, even putting pans of water under the table legs. But nothing could defeat the red ants.

Of course, there were mosquitoes, seemingly millions of them. They attacked this "rich" American with an appetite nothing short of voracious. Their bites turned my legs into a mass of livid sores that never healed until I started my novitiate about nine months after arriving at Mei-shan. The sisters joshed that I had become a novice only because a novice's thick, black, cotton stockings repelled the mosquitoes. Well, to be honest, those stockings were a godsend. They did act as deterrents.

I cannot ignore the lizards, either. The first few times I saw them clinging to the ceiling, I jumped and let out a muffled scream, although everybody assured me that they were harmless. They have their good points, though. They eat mosquitoes. They also have their bad points. Their urine leaves a painful burn on the skin. I was affected that way twice, once on the neck and another time on the eyelid. The second time I became ill from the toxic effects.

Of course, as part of being and living Chinese, there was the food. The diet was basically starchy because of the rice. It was served in some form at every meal. Although I always had plenty to eat, the problem with the food stemmed from the fact that it was bland. To offset this, my stomach began crying for sweets, especially chocolate. Almost all my letters home carried a reminder to send Hershey bars. I made certain to mention that the sisters enjoyed the candy, too, to avoid having Pop and Jo jump to any erroneous conclusions that I was not getting enough to eat.

"That box of Hershey bars you sent went like hot cakes," I wrote in one letter. "The sisters love them. Chinese chocolate is not too good, and they are wild about the American kind. So, please send some more whenever you have a chance. Also, could you include a few cans of Hershey cocoa? There is a soda water here called *ch'i-shui*. It's something like 7-Up. We can make chocolate sodas from the *ch'i-shui* and cocoa."

All of that was true. The sisters did relish American chocolate. So did I, but too much so. My clothes did not fit any more; they stretched at the seams. Some of the sisters who did exquisite needlework pitched in to make the dresses a size or so larger.

My hands and mind were busy, too. Mother Philomena

put me to work right away studying Mandarin. Her philosophy, and it was correct, was that I could not go out alone among the sick until I had mastered the language. Additionally, the long hours of study—as much as ten hours a day—kept my mind occupied. She was aware of that also, as a busy person has an easier time of blending into new surroundings and a radically different culture and way of life. Chinese is not really a difficult language in a grammatical sense because it is stripped down to bare essentials. Such things as verb conjugations are eliminated, for example. The inflections were what bothered me. The slightest shift in tone would change the meaning completely. Luckily for me, Sister Raphael Chan, who was my tutor, was a patient soul while I struggled with the inflections.

I also spent some time with Sister Edna at the clinic, principally to observe ailments and diseases for future reference, and let the patients become accustomed to my presence. One day there was a break in the routine. Word came that a woman was dying of a heart attack at her home two miles away. Sister Edna and I hurried on foot (our principal means of transportation on house calls in those days) through the mountains to discover that she had a mild case of indigestion. Fortunately, it was nothing more than that, and some bicarbonate of soda quickly put her on the road to recovery. Meantime, a letter came from Bette Wang that she was in a hospital and needed an eye operation. Mother Philomena gave me permission to spend a few days with Bette in Taipei. As it turned out, the operation was a false alarm and her eyes responded to medical treatment. When I returned to Mei-shan, I discovered that a mix-up in plans had developed. Somehow, and to this day I do not know how it happened, somebody had the impression that I was to work in a private hospital in another town. Mother Philomena was upset.

So was I; and so were the people at the hospital when they learned they had been misinformed.

And then all of a sudden, Christmas was upon us. Some of the sisters joined the cook in the kitchen to prepare special dishes, such as *chiao-tzu* and *ch'ung-tzu,* the day before Christmas. *Chiao-tzu* is a food from the mainland. It is made by mixing ground pork, rice noodles, garlic and salt. Small portions of the mixture are placed on pieces of thinly-rolled dough, the edges of which are pinched together, like ravioli. These little goodies are then put in a wicker basket and steamed. They are delicious. *Ch'ung-tzu* is a tasty Taiwanese dish. It is made from rice and placed inside young bamboo leaves and steamed.

While the kitchen work was under way, some of the other sisters and I were dispatched into the mountains to find a Christmas tree. We hunted and hunted, but all we could find were scrawny, crooked-trunk pines. We must have walked five miles up and down the mountainside until we came to a farmer's house. The farmer and his family were clinic patients, and they all went along to find a suitable tree. When we did, he chopped it down, and the sisters and I took turns carrying it down the mountain.

The day-long mountain climbing gave me a ravenous appetite. The heady aromas from the kitchen made me want to rush in and grab a handful of the goodies. I realized, probably for the first time in my life, what it meant to be half-starved. When Mother Philomena sent word that I was to join the sisters for dinner for the first time, the significance of her invitation was overshadowed by an overwhelming hunger. I devoured bowls of *chiao-tzu* and *ch'ung-tzu.* No Christmas turkey or duck ever tasted so delicious.

I finally drew a finger across my throat to show that I was full. This was part of the sign language we had developed for communicating. The sisters roared and talked happily. They were delighted that I liked Chinese food. It was further proof that I was sincere in wanting to be Chinese among the Chinese. I believe that did more to break the formality that existed than anything that had happened before or since. Although the sisters had gone out of their way to make me feel at home, I always sensed a reserve. That Christmas Eve helped draw us closer together. It was a warm and comfortable feeling.

About ten o'clock that night, we went to the Our Lady of China Church to get ready for the procession that preceded the midnight mass. The church itself was beautifully decorated. The parishioners had spent the entire day putting up a tree in the nave and trimming it with colorful papier-mâché balls and silver tinsel. It was a work of art with the preciseness and delicacy of Chinese art. There was also a nativity scene.

I was to receive my first lesson in adapting Christianity to the culture of a non-Christian land. On the whole, Taiwan is Buddhist. The population is only approximately four per cent Christian. When the Buddhists observe a feast day, or ask for some special prayer to be answered, they parade the proper god through town. It is, naturally, pomp and ceremony that also includes the gong-gong-gong, clang-clang-clang of bronze cymbals being struck with sticks. The Catholic Church long ago recognized religious processions as an integral part of a country's culture. Thus, on Christmas Eve, Catholics parade with the Christ child statue resting in a sedan. The sedan is made from bamboo, all of which is covered with red, green and white crepe paper. Silver icicles hang from the roof's edges, and under the roof itself glows an eyeball-size lamp from a flashlight. Our Christ child was a beat-up rubber doll that had come in a relief shipment from the United States.

A little after eleven o'clock, Father Sun indicated that the procession should start. Everybody lit a candle, and the parade was on its way from the churchyard and into the street beside the church and mother house. Father Sun led the procession, followed by the sisters, four men carrying the sedan on long, bamboo poles, and the parishioners themselves. It was a beautiful and touching sight. Everybody sang hymns, such as *Silent Night* and *O, Little Town of Bethlehem,* which had been translated into Chinese. The procession went about two blocks, turned around and returned to the church. The Christ child was removed from the sedan and gently placed in the crib. One leg had come off, but even that mishap did not detract from the majestic simplicity of the ceremony.

During the mass as Father Sun started the consecration, firecrackers began blasting away at the church door. I jumped a foot out of the pew. Not only was I frightened, I was shocked at this desecration of the solemnity and holiness of the occasion. Father Sun continued as though nothing were happening. It was not desecration at all; it was simply the Chinese way of celebrating the nineteen hundred and fifty-ninth anniversary of Christ's birth. The firecrackers were their expression of joy, woven into China's culture for many centuries.

Within the Our Lady of China community and the parish as a whole, Christmas was celebrated with all the rich tradition, warmth and gaiety found among Christians everywhere in the world. It was outside the Church itself that there was a marked difference. The little business district of Mei-shan had no decorated yule trees in the town square, or strings of lights over the street, or Santa Clauses in the stores. In Chiayi City, a busy metropolis of a quarter million people and only about fifteen miles from Mei-shan, there was also a dearth of the Christmas spirit as I knew it back home. There were no shoppers, their arms laden with packages wrapped in red and green, scurrying in and out of stores; no recorded Christmas carols being played in the stores; no huge window displays of Santa Claus in his workshop with the elves and all making toys. Occasionally, there would be a little display of Christmas greeting cards in both Chinese and English. Some pictured the nativity scene. Some were of the Currier and Ives' rural, snow-scene variety, which seemed very much out of place. The weather in Chiayi was warm, as the city is astride the Tropic of Cancer. And on Christmas Day, there was business as usual.

Within our own community, though, the holiday season threw everything out of kilter. It brimmed with the same eager, gay spirit that existed back home; nobody really had his heart fully in the normal, everyday chores. Language lessons began to drag and were even interrupted on the slightest pretext. Letters I had planned to write to the family and friends were put aside until after the New Year.

There was still another distraction during this period. Bishop Niu gave the sisters his bicycle. It was the first means of transportation they had owned in Taiwan. So, it created quite a stir within the convent. I had never seen nuns riding a bicycle, and it struck me funny watching them struggling with the hems of their habits and trying to keep their balance. Most of the sisters had never ridden a bicycle. As a result, they were sprawled on the ground as much as they were upright on the bike. Luckily, there were no casualties, except some bruised shoulders and elbows and skinned fingers.

The bicycle riding was another way of communicating with the sisters. Laughter and sign language came into play. We had a barrel of fun. It helped cement our friendship, which, in turn, brought us closer together in the family spirit that prevailed within the community.

It was hard for me, an automobile-oriented American, to understand why the sisters placed so much value on that bicycle and learning to ride it. I had picked up enough

Chinese to catch such expressions as, "We won't have to walk," or "God is being good to our feet." As yet, I had not had to do too much walking over the rugged, back-country, mountain roads. Thus, a bike was still something for kids, at least in my eyes. But this was no child's play for the sisters. While they laughed and had a lot of fun developing a sense of balance while at the same time learning to keep the hems of their habits from catching in the sprocket, there was, nonetheless, a deadly serious-ness about their desire to learn to ride and an attitude that the bike was a prized possession. As time went on, and I started to make house calls alone in distant places, I began to understand what they meant. It saved an aw-fully lot of wear and tear on feet.

The bicycle was only part of my adjustment to Chinese life. Mother Philomena wasted no time in hastening it. There were bus trips to Chiayi City, which sat on the fer-tile plains that extended westward to the coast of the Straits of Taiwan. A week before Christmas, some of the sisters took me to a church dedication at Chico, a little town about twenty miles from Mei-shan. There was a holiday atmosphere about the town. Although only two per cent of the population was Catholic, it seemed that all the towns-people turned out to take part in the ceremonies and also to welcome Bishop Niu, who presided at the dedication. Of course, there were the firecrackers going bang-bang-bang before, during and after mass. I was the only West-erner there, and, naturally, attracted attention. Especially my nose. One little girl reached up and touched it, then ran off laughing. I was a *ch'ang-pi-tzu*, all right.

As still another part of the introduction to Chinese life, a few of the sisters took me to a Buddhist temple atop the mountain back of the mother house. This was a mile walk up a twisting, uneven road that was sometimes rocky and sometimes overgrown with grass. I was from good old flatland Illinois, and mountain climbing was not one of my strong points. I fell most of the way up and down. (I also had trouble getting used to the open gutters along the curbless sidewalks in towns and cities. Once, I stepped right into one, much to my embarrassment and Mother Philomena's consternation. I think she aged ten years until I finally learned how to walk in the mountains and avoid teetering on the edge of open gutters.)

When we finally reached the temple, it was worth all the tripping and stumbling. It was true Chinese architecture: the red tile roof flared gracefully outward from the top of each story, while the main roof itself swept elegantly upward into a sharp backbone that ran the length of the temple. Some of the *ni-ku*, Buddhist nuns, were outside throwing pieces of wood into the air. I thought at first that the *ni-ku* were men. Their heads were shaved and the pates glistened in the bright December sun. They wore knee-length coats and pantaloons that looked more like baggy trousers. The pieces of wood they threw were flat on one side and rounded on the other; they were small, about the size of a bluepoint oyster. The *ni-ku* flipped two at a time. When one landed flat and the other round, the thrower seemed pleased and threw no more. It appeared to be a game. I found out later that it definitely was not that at all. This was a serious business in which the *ni-ku* asked the gods to bring them good luck. It reminded me, in a way, of a practice young swains engaged in back home with flowers, picking the petals until finally one flower came out, "she loves me."

There was a terrible letdown after the holidays as life at the convent went back to normal. I returned to long hours of language study. In the weeks before Christmas and the New Year holidays, I had attacked the lessons with all the zest of a bright-eyed, eager freshman student. Now they were a drudge and my mind went blank as soon as I opened a book or picked up a pen to practice drawing the intricate characters that make up the written language. Walks into the village lost their appeal; the sameness of the architecture and the small, hole-in-the-wall stores became monotonous. There was not a drugstore where I could get a Coke, or a chocolate soda, or a chocolate sundae. That yearning for sweets, especially chocolate to offset the bland diet, was becoming unbearable. If only I could get a juicy steak and a cold, heaping dish of ice cream!

A psychological problem also developed over the meals. Mother Philomena insisted on my having four eggs for breakfast and pork or fowl at one other meal at least. The sisters' Spartan diet seldom included those foods for the simple reason that they were too expensive. Although I rarely ate eggs in the States and told her that, she insisted that I needed the protein nourishment.

"All Americans eat eggs and meat all the time," she maintained. "We Chinese are accustomed to a different diet. We can be healthy on it, but you cannot."

I tried to explain, but to no avail, that she had a misconception about Americans and their diets. I also argued strongly against this preferential treatment. For one thing, the Our Lady of China community was in no position to spend money for extras. For another, I wanted to eat what the others did as part of my desire to live Chinese. Also, I began to worry that the sisters as a whole would become resentful about my special meals. They never did, by the way. In fact, they sided with their superior general that Westerners could not stay healthy on a Chinese diet.

Meantime, the weather turned chillier, particularly at night. With no heat in the mother house, I nearly froze to death in this bone-chilling, damp climate. The sisters poured hot water into bottles that I hugged to my stomach. Catholic Relief Services-N.C.W.C. in the United States came through, too, with a shipment of clothing. It was for distribution among the needy. I borrowed three overcoats, temporarily of course. And used all three, plus the bottles filled with hot water at the same time. Only then did I feel reasonably comfortable. Even so, I longed to be able to walk into a steam-heated house. There was no such thing among the Chinese in our area.

Aside from the indigestion "emergency" case before Christmas, I had done hardly any medical work in the first six weeks. I started to believe that my talents were being wasted, and worried whether they would become rusty. Surely, I reasoned, there must be something to do where the language barrier would not interfere. I almost kissed Sister Raphael Kuo when she asked me to accompany her on some house calls far back in the mountains. The journey was to be made on foot, as usual, but I did not care. Sister Kuo had some training in nursing. She said, in slow and simple Chinese, that there was one patient in particular she wanted me to see. Perhaps there was something I could do. The patient was a young mother of three children. She was in her twenties and had tuberculosis. The disease had killed her parents and her husband. Relatives had taken the children away from her, but only one relative would do personal chores for this poor soul. At first, it was difficult to understand this reluctance. After a while, I found out that among the Chinese, and especially the rural Taiwanese, tuberculosis was a dreaded word. To them it signified certain death, and close contact with a tubercular person was tantamount to signing their own death warrant. The relatives, then, had left her to die. The one who did try to help was scared to death and visited the patient no more than once a week. The children, of course, were never permitted to see their mother.

The woman lived in a one-room, mud and bamboo shack, the back of which sat on the mountainside and the front on stilts. An old, rickety, bamboo ladder led up to the narrow, low front door. In the dimness of the windowless room, I could make out a form lying on a thin, straw pallet stretched over the wood floor. Close up, she wore an old, faded kimono. Her sunken face was pasty. She wore no stockings or shoes; her legs were skin and bones. I thought she was dead until Sister Kuo spoke and a thin smile edged the woman's bluish lips. I had never seen anything so heartbreaking as this sight. It turned my stomach. She lay there, not a sound, not a whimper, no tears. She just lay there, too weak to get up, and patiently waited to die.

Sister Raphael got down on her knees beside the woman, took some food from her small, black satchel, lifted the woman's head and began to feed her. I had never seen such compassion and gratitude as in the tableau they created: Sister Kuo patiently feeding this nearly dead woman and talking softly to her; the woman reaching far back into her body for the strength to chew the food, smiling all the while. There were some vitamins in my medical kit. I gave her one and left a half dozen in a paper envelope within arm's reach and oral instructions to take three a day until we returned. The sisters made every effort to see her at least three times a week, to feed and bathe her and clean the shack. Their own manpower was spread so thin in so many endeavors that visiting the woman thrice weekly was a tremendous burden on them. Yet, they went without fail.

Their efforts were solely humanitarian, but, regretfully, not therapeutic. The woman needed immediate hospitalization, although it was late for a cure. A hospital bed would have meant at least some comfort in her waning days. There were, however, no free, public tuberculosis sanatoriums and the provincial hospital could admit only a few such patients because of the prohibitive cost of long-time care. Few people could afford it. This woman most definitely could not. I had a sudden and wild dream. If our community could have its own hospital this woman could have the care she needed and deserved. Moreover, the hospital would free the sisters for other duties rather than day-long trips for visits. I quickly returned to the reality of no hospital being available. Surely, there had to be some way of treating her.

All the way back to Mei-shan, three names repeatedly ran through my mind. INAH, PAS and streptomycin. I knew that these drugs could save lives. They were the miracle drugs in the field of tuberculosis. Was there any at the convent's clinic? If not, where could some be obtained quickly? Vitamins? Yes, they were fine; they would help build up resistance to fight the tuberculosis, but they would fall far short of the cure. INAH, PAS, streptomycin. They had to be found to help others in the Our Lady of China community's area. I went directly into the little clinic and began searching through bottles and boxes. There was nothing that could help. (I later found some INAH and streptomycin buried in an out-of-the-way place.) The paucity of our medical supplies struck home once again. I was heartsick and sat down on a little stool, put my head in my hands and broke down.

There I was with years of medical training, specialized through a degree in public health at Marquette University, but hardly anything to work with. I do not mean patients in that sense. We had dozens of them; we could treat hundreds if we had the proper medications. There were such diseases as tuberculosis, cancer, polio, trachoma, skin diseases, dysentery, anemia (including the usually fatal aplastic anemia), palsy, heart ailments, worms, goiters, kidney ailments, leprosy, ulcers, leukemia, and malnutrition.

As the names of the sicknesses ran through my mind, great and serious doubts arose. What good would I be if there was no medicine? The community could not afford the hundreds of dollars, a bare minimum at best, to stock the clinic with an adequate supply of even the most essential drugs. Moreover, there was no place I knew of that would provide them both free *and* quickly. Six months, nine months perhaps before the requisitions to charitable agencies in the United States could be processed and the drugs' arrival here at Mei-shan. That was an eternity. Meantime, why should I stay here and do no more than bandage some cuts, or take some food and vitamins to somebody who would die anyhow because proper medicine was not available? That would be a deliberate and unnecessary waste of years of education. There had to be someplace in the Far East where I could do some good, a place that had plenty of medicines. Either that, or better still, go home and settle down. Mei-shan, romantic-sounding Plum Mountain, was a bust, a complete washout. Maybe the rest of the Orient was that way, too. Or, more correctly, maybe I was not emotionally geared to the exacting life of a lay missionary in any country where the culture and living and health standards were entirely foreign to those of my own. I had been warned that life out here would be harsh. It was far more so than I had ever imagined.

After having dinner in my room, I joined the sisters relaxing in the sitting room. I tried to cover my feelings with light talk in my sorely limited Chinese. It was an unsuccessful attempt. Mother Philomena watched me carefully. Sister Raphael paid more attention than normal. Not so much in words as in glances. There was an uneasiness in the air. Some of the sisters talked among themselves and I could not catch any of the words. It was obvious that they were using the Taiwanese dialect, and I realized that their conversation was about me. I did not like being talked about without an opportunity to answer, and I wanted to run out of the sitting room and back to my room and think out my problems and future plans. I excused myself as gracefully as possible.

In the States, I had a built-in companion for moods of depression when big and serious problems came up. It was a record player. I would put on a stack of Broadway musicals, or a piano concerto, stretch out on the bed and let the music calm my emotions so that I could think clearly. It never failed to help. Here at Mei-shan, there was no record player. There were only some books, and a few letters waiting for answers. I was in no mood to write bright replies to Pop and Jo back home to keep their minds at ease that everything was going fine. I was not really in the mood for books, either, although I thumbed through them and finally picked up Canon Jacques LeClerq's biography of Father Lebbe, *Thunder in the Distance*. I had read excerpts in pamphlet form at Crossroads Students Center in Chicago and found great comfort from Father Lebbe's turbulent life of frustrations. On the boat to Taiwan, I had the full book and read parts of it, particularly the story of the two European women, Sisters Luke and Chow, who became Chinese with the Chinese on the mainland. I wondered if rereading their story would help me. My thoughts were interrupted by a light tapping on the door. The visitor, whoever it was, was not welcome; I wanted to be alone.

"Who is it?" I finally asked and walked to the screen door. Sister Raphael Chan was there.

"May I come in?"

Her words startled me. I must have gone to the door and just stood there and stared. "Yes, certainly." I hastened to push open the door. I motioned for her to use the chair while I sat on the edge of the bed.

"It is a beautiful night," she said. "Have you seen the stars? They are like diamonds in the sky."

I sensed that Sister Raphael did not come to my room to discuss the stars or the beauty of the night. Rather, she was being thoroughly and properly Chinese: much polite talk about many, many things before getting down to the purpose of the visit an hour or so later. For once, I wanted to say, be like the Americans for a change; they get right to the heart of the matter. Just what do you want? To find out why I am feeling so blue? But I was in Taiwan, and it would have been highly improper not to follow the good manners of conversation.

"Yes, Sister, I have seen the stars," I said. "They are, as you pictured them, like diamonds."

She nodded and smiled. When I said no more, she calmly picked up the conversation. "I have heard that on nights like this, there is no place in the world so beautiful as Sun Moon Lake. I have heard that the stars are so bright and big that you can reach out and almost touch them. I have heard that there is also the soft background of the wind whispering in the big, majestic pine trees that flourish there. Someday, perhaps you and I can go and see and hear for ourselves. It is not too far from here, but there has been little time for sight-seeing. Would you like to make the trip?"

The question was a deft probing to find out whether I planned to leave the community soon. I sidestepped it: "It does sound beautiful," and said no more.

"It is beautiful, Gloria, but we should wait another month, until February, when the warm weather returns. The mountains will be filled with orchids and lilies. They grow wild and you can pick all you want. Is it true that they are very costly in the United States?"

The conversation dragged on and on like that, about this beautiful place and that beautiful place in Taiwan, and then into the gaiety of the Chinese New Year celebration. "It is most unfortunate that so few Westerners ever see this pageantry except once in a while in the big cities. Here, in the small towns and villages, we are close to the people; we see them sewing and cooking and preparing in many, many ways. It is all so worthwhile seeing."

I wondered when she would ever get down to the real purpose of her visit. But she arose and started for the door. "It is getting late," she said. "Also, I have taken up much of your time, and I apologize for having been so rude when you no doubt had many things to do. The book, for instance," and she pointed to the Father Lebbe biography on the table. "Reading is good. Books can be great friends. They can bring peace of mind."

I suddenly understood her message: do not be hasty in any decisions. Read, travel on the island; everything is not ugly here; there is much beauty and much gaiety. Hers was the most oblique approach I had ever encountered.

Sister Raphael turned toward me just as she reached the door. "Gloria, we are poor now. It has not always been that way with us, as you know from the stories we have told about China. It will not be always that way, either. We pray, all of us pray very hard; we offer novenas constantly. One day, God will answer us."

"I am certain that He will," I said.

Sister Raphael studied me for a few moments. "Gloria, you can do much good here. We all love you, and we need you. The people need you, too. They also like and trust you." With that, she opened the door and walked into the night.

I was stunned. How did she know that I had actually given thought to going away? How did anybody know what was on my mind?

"Sister Raphael," I called out. She stopped and looked back. I went out to her side. "You are trying to tell me not to leave, but how did you know what I was thinking?"

"No, you did not say that. You did not have to. But we knew. Your face was sad, perhaps because of what you saw today, or perhaps because of the quiet life here. But that is not all. Your eyes were far, far away, in another land."

I bit my lower lip to help choke back the tears. "I have been dishonest with myself," I finally said.

Sister Raphael shook her head, puzzled. "I do not understand what you mean. You are not a dishonest person."

"Someday I will explain what I mean. Right now, I don't think I can talk about it very well, or rather, explain it so that it makes any sense."

As I prepared for bed, my thoughts centered on the agreement I had made with myself that first night at Meishan: stay for six months before making a decision. I had almost broken that pact. I stretched full-length on the straw pallet before twisting and turning to find a comfortable position. The creaking straw gave off a sound that I had not noticed before, like crickets chirping in a forest. It was soothing, almost like the pattering of rain on a tin roof. Rain, wouldn't that be wonderful! No more bucket brigades to the village well. Maybe we would have our own well, and a pump, and hot showers, and—I think I chuckled a little, but I am not certain because everything became fuzzier and fuzzier and fuzzier in the encroaching sleep.

CHAPTER FOUR

The Sisters of Our Lady of China had not always been a struggling, hand-to-mouth community. The early days on mainland China were quite the contrary. Thomas Cardinal Tien,* S.V.D., started the community in the Province of Shantung in northeastern China. The Little Sisters of St. Teresa, established by Father Lebbe, helped Cardinal Tien lay the foundation. Our Lady of China was strictly a Chinese community. Until I was permitted to join, it had never had anybody but Chinese in the membership. The sisters had a comfortable mother house in the rural city of Kaotang, not far from the Yellow River. Aspirants were many, and those chosen were carefully picked for vocations and sent on to school for further education. The sisters themselves taught in schools, did catechistical and social service work, and administered to the sick as nurses. Even though they were in the midst of war (Japan had occupied their part of China), they were able to flourish to some extent. Their numbers grew until there were forty professed sisters, novices and aspirants by the time World War II began drawing to a close in 1945.

* Thomas Cardinal Tien founded the Sisters of Our Lady of China when he was Bishop of the Yangku diocese. When he received his Red Hat in 1946, he became the first and only Chinese Cardinal in the Catholic Church. After his escape from the Chinese Communists, he spent some time in the United States before his appointment as Apostolic Administrator of the Archdiocese of Taipei in 1960. He retired in May, 1966.

When the tide of war turned against the Japanese, every-body eagerly awaited the liberation and the return of the Nationalist Government of Generalissimo Chiang Kai-shek. With the liberation, it was believed that strongly en-trenched pockets of Communists in the area also would be dislodged. This hope was to be doomed. Their armies had gobbled up huge chunks of China in the north and east. Although the Japanese were no friends to the religious groups, the Communists were even harsher in their treat-ment. They pronounced the death sentence on Cardinal Tien. They did likewise with Bishop Niu, who had become the Bishop of the Yangku diocese when Cardinal Tien re-ceived his Red Hat and was assigned to Peiping. Cardinal Tien and Bishop Niu were among the many religious who were able to escape.

Even so, the Sisters of Our Lady of China hoped they would be permitted to go on with their work. It soon be-came obvious that they, too, were under a death sentence. Nothing so crude as a firing squad. Rather, something sub-tle, such as being worked to death.

The sisters were naturally reticent about recounting their frightful days with the Communists and their terror-filled, torturous escape that eventually took them to Mei-shan. The period was something they wanted to forget. I was with the community six years before I was able, finally, to piece together this part of their lives. Even then, sixteen years after they had reached the safety of Hong Kong, the deep-seated terror of that era showed in their eyes and faces, and cropped up in quickened breathing whenever they recalled harrowing incidents. One evening, for ex-ample, while I was developing material for this book, Sisters Catherine Chang and Raphael Kuo turned pale as they recalled a case of a gatekeeper and blind boy being beaten into unconsciousness by the Communists who had accused them of a crime they had not committed. That had happened more than eighteen years before. Yet the incident was still as fresh in their memories as though it had happened that day.

As is customary within all communities of nuns, the Sisters of Our Lady of China were stationed in different parts of the Yangku diocese in China. A few did clinic work at Yangku, some were in nurses' training at the archdiocese hospital in Tsinan. Others, along with the novices, postulants and aspirants, were at the mother house in Kaotang. The latter, west of the Yellow River, was on the northwestern corner of a roughly shaped diamond formed by four cities. Yangku, also west of the river, was at the southwestern corner; Tsinan, east of the river, was at the northeastern point; and Yenchou at the southeastern corner. The perimeter covered more than 200 miles. This was Japanese-held territory at that time, although the Communists managed to infiltrate and grow stronger as the tide of World War II turned against the Japanese. The Japanese in the area gave the sisters little trouble because the Catholics there were under the religious guidance of German missionaries from the Society of the Divine Word. By the end of the war, in the summer of 1945, much of Shantung province had become a Communist stronghold. Kaotang and Yangku became Communist-held cities. Tsinan and Yenchou remained in Nationalist Government hands, although there were bands of Communists in the nearby mountains.

It was only natural that when the atheistic Communists moved in, religious groups became prime targets for persecution. The thirty nuns, novices, postulants and aspirants at the mother house in Kaotang were harassed day and night. They were pulled from the compound to care for the sick and wounded at all hours. They got little rest. They were put on a starvation diet uncountable times when the Communists confiscated their meager food supplies. They were called individually and in groups before Communist committees for interrogation and brainwashing.

"You spy for the Kuomintang (the Chinese Nationalist Party)," they were told. A denial fell on deaf ears.

"You collaborated with the Japanese," and again denial was brushed aside. The charges went on and on.

"You believe in God?"

"Yes."

"You are crazy. We will change that."

The harassment dragged on through 1946 and 1947. The sisters and candidates were subjected to brainwashing sessions that lasted through the long nights and then, their brains numb and muscles aching from fatigue, they were ordered back to work during the day with the sick and war-maimed. Finally, they were called before the local committee and told they could not wear their habits.

"You will get rid of that capitalist clothing and wear the people's garments," the party chairman decreed.

They were no more or less fortunate than three sisters at the community's clinic in Yangku. Two of them survived, Sisters Catherine Chang and Raphael Kuo. The third, Sister Gabriel Wang, was one of those worked to death.

"The Communists ordered us to go to Yangku when Sister Gabriel was dying," Sister Catherine told me one night as we sat with Sister Raphael Kuo. "The Communists there started to do the same to us as they did at Kaotang. We would work all day and into the evening. We would fall in bed at ten or eleven o'clock at night, and would be awakened within an hour to go back to work. When the bombers came during the day, we would run with the rest of the people and soldiers and take shelter in foxholes. The Communists would ridicule us, hollering, 'Where is your God now!' and things like that. Then they would point their guns at us and force us to go back into the clinic while the bombing went on.

"Some of the people warned us that the Communists were going to parade us through the entire district—to make a spectacle out of us," Sister Raphael Kuo said. "Then we were to be put on trial as enemies of the people and sentenced to work in a hospital someplace far away in the West. The people also told us that we would go through brainwashing. They warned us to leave quickly, but we were so confused that we did not know what to do. We tried to get a message through to the convent at Kaotang, but it never reached the sisters. Every time we turned around, somebody would quietly warn us to leave. One night we prayed for divine guidance. The next day a stranger came and said, 'Sisters, the people have told me to help you cross the Yellow River and into the Government's sector. Are you willing to go?'"

They were advised to discard their habits in favor of Chinese-type baggy pantaloons and loose blouses to make themselves inconspicuous, and also be ready to leave at three o'clock in the morning.

"When the time arrived and I said, 'Let's go,' we were both so frightened that we shook all over," Sister Catherine recalled. "We were so scared we could hardly move. When the gatekeeper saw us, we told him that we were going on an emergency call. We thought this would save him from trouble. We heard later that the Communists beat him and also the little blind boy who lived at the clinic. The Communists accused them of plotting to help our escape."

The two nuns met their guide at a pre-arranged spot and began walking through the fields. They walked until daybreak before taking a rest. The roads swarmed with Communist soldiers checking everybody going through. The nuns and their companion kept to the fields. Even there, they were in constant fright as they encountered scores of others trudging in all directions. Fortunately, none was a Communist. Blisters formed and broke on their feet, leaving huge, bleeding sores. Their progress was slowed to a painfully hobbling pace. In the first week, when they reached the temporary sanctuary of a Catholic family, they had covered less than fifteen of the seventy-five miles to their destination in Tsinan. Actually, they had walked closer to fifty miles because of the zig-zag routes necessary to avoid Communist troops and checkpoints.

"We were with the family only two days when they were warned that the Communists had picked up our trail," Sister Catherine recalled. "We had to leave quickly. We knew that we were never any further than ten miles from the Yellow River, but our guide said it was not safe to cross yet, that we would have to go farther.

"Sometimes, when there were no soldiers in sight, we would walk along a road with thousands of other refugees. Then the Communists would send planes to strafe the roads and scare people from leaving. We would jump into ditches. Some of them were drainage ditches and we would be covered with muck. Many times we hid for days in barns and groves of trees to avoid search parties. Many, many other times we had to turn back and make a swing dozens of miles out of the way when rumors reached us that the Communists had set up checkpoints or were combing the villages and fields for refugees.

"We really did not know how long we had been walking, maybe four, maybe five months before we came to a place our guide said was safe for the river crossing. We remembered that the weather had turned cold. We had fortunately taken our habits apart and sewn the pieces inside the pantaloons and blouses. That helped keep us a little warm, except at night when it was too dangerous to have a fire and the cold would bury itself in our bones."

Food was a luxury. Every now and then a family would give the two nuns a bowl of yellow rice, which, at that time, was more plentiful than flour in the wheat-growing

northland of China. Other refugees sometimes would share
some yellow rice, or watery rice soup. Grass and tree roots
became a part of the subsistence. Once in a while their
guide appeared with a chicken or a duck. They never asked
questions, but surmised that he had invaded some barn-
yard under the cover of darkness. Their bodies turned thin,
and their clothing, already in tatters, hung like limp rags.
There were days when they were too weak to travel, and
they hid out in the fields or small clusters of trees, prayer-
fully hopeful that they would escape detection, not only
by the Communist troops but by farmers and villagers seeking to curry favor with the enemy.

At the Yellow River crossing, the boatman told the sisters
and their guide that the Communists had refused permission for any more boats to cross to the Nationalist side.
The guide, meanwhile, had arranged for forged papers tes-
tifying that the sisters were from a high-ranking Communist
family. Until then, they had been afraid to use the passes
in case they would be recognized as forgeries. That would
have meant facing a firing squad. But now they had to take
that risk. Apparently, the boatman was impressed because
at 11:30 that night, he rowed them over, and without charge.

"The boatman must have thought we were infiltrators
and was afraid to charge us anything because we were
'relatives' of such high-placed Communists," Sister Raphael
Kuo chuckled.

When they crawled out of the boat, they sank to their
knees in mud. There were no lanterns, no torches, no artificial light of any kind on the moonless night, as they were
in the heart of a heavily contested war zone. The mud immediately pulled the shoes off their feet. They staggered
barefoot for hours before they reached dry land in the first
light of the cold dawn. They collapsed, unable to move
another step. Their legs and feet were badly swollen and
cut. Blood oozed through the thick coating of yellow mud.

They lay there, half conscious, the entire day. The bone-chilling cold of the oncoming night forced them to get up and move on in search of shelter. They had not realized it, but they were only a few hundred yards from a village and a sanctuary with a Catholic family. Half-dead from starvation and the extreme cold, they gulped steaming bowls of tea and yellow rice. The nourishment and the house's warmth partially revived them.

"Is there a priest we could see to have a mass said?" they asked. They had not heard mass since leaving Yangku six months before. The family immediately made arrangements for a priest to come that night.

"That family was so kind that we felt right at home," Sister Catherine said. "They helped bathe our legs and dress our cuts. We stayed there for nearly a week before we were able to move on. Then they arranged for a farmer to let us have a cow cart to carry us to Tsinan, about ten miles away."

In Tsinan, they went directly to the diocesan hospital, certain that the other sisters stationed there would have news from the mother house in Kaotang. They were stunned to hear that the mother house had been closed and that all the sisters and candidates had fled Kaotang months before, but were delighted to know they were safe in Tsinan. There was a joyous reunion, as everybody was certain that Sisters Catherine and Raphael had suffered the same fate as Sister Gabriel Wang. The Kaotang group had been more fortunate. They reached Tsinan, fifty miles away, in ten days, traveling mostly on foot. Like the two nuns from Yangku, they, too, had forged papers to get them across the Yellow River.

Also like the Yangku sisters, they had had many harrowing problems with the Communists, especially the soldiers who made daily and sometimes thrice daily inspections of the mother house and the community's clinic. The Communist sick and wounded demanded VIP treatment. If the sisters were without proper medicine, they were accused of selling it or hoarding it for the rich. A group of soldiers arrived with a fungus infection. When they were told there was no medicine for this in the depleted stocks, they threatened to arrest the sisters for black marketeering. Some of the nuns quickly thought of another treatment, alcohol and also salt mixed with water. The soldiers came back the next day, pleased with the remedy. The sisters explained that they would have to go to a larger city to get new supplies that would heal the fungus much faster.

In fact, it was that pretext that helped them escape. Father John B. Hu, Bishop Niu's representative, arranged for forged transit papers. The sisters hitched up their cow to a cart donated by a Catholic family. The work- and hunger-weakened sisters rode in the cart. The stronger ones went on foot. Those who could not use the medication pretext slipped away during the night, hurrying as fast and far as their feet would take them before they hid in caves at dawn.

Their days in Tsinan were numbered. The Communists had begun closing in. A month after the reunion, the sisters had to pack up again and start on foot to Yenchou, sixty miles to the south. Before they left, three sisters volunteered to stay on at the hospital and timed their own flight for the moment the Communists arrived. The take-over caught them by surprise and they were trapped at their posts. To the best of anybody's knowledge, they were never able to leave Tsinan. The other sisters, meanwhile, went on to Yenchou and found a haven with the Holy Ghost Sisters. They sent a letter to Father Hu in Nanking of their whereabouts and found work as embroiderers in a vestment factory to earn money for food.

After helping the sisters escape from Kaotang, Father Hu had gone on to Nanking. He had had no easy time himself in reaching the Nationalist Government capital. He was on the road, mostly on foot, more than five months. Like so many others, escape for him was mandatory as he had been sentenced to death.

"It was Epiphany and very cold when I arrived in Nanking," Father Hu recalled during one of my visits with him in Taipei, where he is Cardinal Tien's representative. "An American priest asked if I would like to have some American military clothing. I took two suits. They were beautiful. I immediately got very warm. I wrote to the sisters to come to Nanking as Archbishop Yupin* would give me a parish and they could work in it. Also, it was safer in Nanking, and the Archbishop gave me permission to go north for them.

"At that time, the government controlled the railroad lines, but there were Communists on both sides and fighting every day. The railroad carried only soldiers—no civilians. I was a 'soldier' in my uniform. Everybody told me—priests and sisters who had come down from the north—that civilians could not get into Yenchou. When the train came into Yenchou, I saw some fellow and said, 'Here, take my bag.' I walked just like a leader, and nobody stopped me. I saw the sisters and told them to get ready to leave the next day.

"The sisters were upset. They said some people were urging them to give up, to disband and go back to their homes. I told them, 'No, you must stay together. Cardinal Tien, who is my good friend, started your community and I will help you. Some day all of this will be over and everything will be fine again.' They were relieved and began gathering their belongings.

"The poor sisters had nothing. They had been in Yenchou only a month, not sufficient time to earn enough money to

* The Most Rev. Paul Yupin, Archbishop of Nanking. He is now president of Fukien University in Taiwan.

refurnish their wardrobes. They had just a few odds and ends that could be put in a cloth and wrapped up. They also had a little chair. I asked them to get rid of it, as we would have enough trouble getting on the train without extra burdens like a chair. But they said no, they had brought it from the mother house and intended to keep it. I guess you can call it a sentimental memento. Well, we went to the depot the next day, but there were no passenger trains. There were, I think, twenty-five—fifteen sisters and the others novices and aspirants. I saw a freight train and there was an open car. It did not have a roof. It was a flatbed car, the kind used in China to transport horses. We all crawled into the car. The train took four days and nights to go to Nanking. Maybe 500 miles. We did not have anything to eat except some *man-t'ou,* steamed bread, that is, and peanuts."

The Our Lady of China group stayed in Nanking while Father Hu went on to Shanghai to get them clothing from Catholic welfare.

"There was no money," he said. "I borrowed money from friends, but they had very little for themselves, and I also worked on a Catholic magazine. There really was not enough money to feed them adequately. They had nothing but rice for about four months. No meat. None at all for four months. The poor sisters were thin. Each one had lost about ten or twelve pounds."

Archbishop Yupin reactivated a parish near Nanking and assigned Father Hu and the Our Lady of China community to work there. Because of the war with Japan, the parish had had no priest for seven years. The church, rectory and convent were in disrepair. Doors were loose, or off; windows were out. Father Hu and the sisters pitched in to make the buildings usable and livable again. The sisters opened a clinic and things went along smoothly for nearly a year when the Communists began moving in. It was time to pack up and flee again; the nightmarish days were back. When they reached Wuhu, some fifty miles southwest of Nanking, a few of the sisters were too ill to go on. It was there that they met Dr. Hyla S. Watters, who treated them without charge at the Methodist Hospital. They finally arrived in Shanghai after nineteen months and more than a 1,000 miles of zig-zag wandering. Boat transportation was arranged to Foochow. This destination, they believed, would definitely be the end of their journey.

But no. They were told to leave Foochow within days after their arrival in the late spring of 1949. They hurried to a small town called Santuao, about forty miles away and a rallying point for some Chinese Catholic priests fleeing the on-coming Communists. There, the Sisters of Our Lady of China met Father Peter A. Kuo. Father Kuo and Mother Philomena had been next-door neighbors and playmates as children. He, too, was now a refugee. He advised the group to hurry to Mawei, a small coastal town near Foochow, and get what reportedly was the last boat leaving that part of Nationalist China for Hong Kong and a rendezvous with Father Hu, who had gone on to Hong Kong to join the faculty of Rosary Hill Seminary. They waited and waited in Mawei, but no boat came. The sisters were frantic. Father Kuo, who had gone along with them, hurried off each morning to the shipping company's office and joined lines of others eagerly in search of news. When the boat steamed into the bay, it anchored a few hundred yards off-shore. The captain said the boat was already overcrowded and he would not take on any more passengers. Father Kuo ignored this message. He put the sisters in a rowboat and got them aboard secretly for the 500-mile trip to Hong Kong. They were totally unaware, as they clambered aboard, that they were only 150 miles from what was to become their home two years later—Taiwan.

Hong Kong was enervatingly hot, and teeming with hundreds of thousands of refugees from Communist China. The sisters and novices—there were only fourteen now, as others had either died or given up from sheer fatigue along the way—arrived with a few bundles of old shoes and old clothing, and a prayer that somehow this would be the end of what had become an aimless, heartbreaking journey of 2,000 miles, half of it on foot, that seemed to be leading them to nowhere in particular. Father Hu met them at the dock. He shepherded them to a room he had been fortunate enough to find in the horribly overcrowded city. Bishop Niu had sent along money for the rent. The room was only about ten feet by eighteen feet, and eight feet to the ceiling. Small as it was for fourteen people, it was palatial against what they had been used to and compared also to living space available in Hong Kong. With the help of some seminarians, Father Hu built a "second floor"—a sleeping platform that was barely more than a shallow cave two feet or so under the ceiling. A policeman investigating living conditions ordered it taken down. The sisters complied—to a point. Each morning they did take it down. But each night they put the boards back, crawled up into the cave and went to sleep.

They had little money for food. Father Hu was able to scrimp and save some; the sisters and novices crocheted doilies and sold them, and took in washing and ironing. The proceeds provided them with a daily diet of a bowl of rice and two bowls of thin, watery rice soup. Nothing else. Their future was as bleak as their diet, as conditions in Hong Kong daily became more discouraging because of the deluge of refugees coming out of China. At the end of nine months, Father Hu arranged with a priest in Macao for the worn-out community to go on to that Portuguese, and predominately Catholic, colony a few hours by boat from Hong Kong. Maybe, just maybe, there would be a future there. Their quarters were larger; their diet was a little better because Catholic families occasionally gave them eggs and meat. Yet, Macao, too, was feeling the effects of the swarm of Chinese refugees, and the sisters were able to do no more than needlework, washing and ironing to help support themselves. Father Hu visited them twice a month, bringing some money and also hearing confessions and teaching vocations. In spite of his help, it was obvious that the Our Lady of China community had little, if any, future.

And then one day, in the summer of 1951, four years after they had fled Shantung province, Bishop Niu was able to send word to join him in Taiwan. There was a promise that the community would be able to start a new life.

They almost never reached Taiwan. Their boat, a small, coastal freighter, ran into a typhoon. It was reported lost, with no survivors. Preparations for a funeral mass were under way in Taipei when the freighter, its radio out, limped into Keelung four days late and discharged its battered cargo of humanity. It included a dozen nuns and novices,* drenched to the skin and sick from the tempestuous voyage. Bishop Niu, however, had a house waiting for them in Hsinchu, about thirty miles from Taipei.

A house. True, it was an old, wooden building that was slowly rotting away, and there were only three small rooms on the first floor and a like number on the second floor. Moreover, it was not in any sense compatible with the usual regulations calling for a convent, novitiate and all the other buildings that make up a mother house complex for nuns, novices and candidates. But these were not usual times, and nobody was going to debate rules and regulations. Especially the Sisters of Our Lady of China who had

---

* Another nun, Sister Catherine Chang, escaped that part of the misery as she had been sent on to the United States to begin studies in chemistry and X ray. The fourteenth nun resigned.

not had anything so spacious in four years. They joyfully resumed parish work, teaching and nursing.

They dreamed of having a feast to celebrate their good fortune of being not just alive but actually remaining together as the Our Lady of China community. They regarded the fact that they were still a community as a God-given privilege. Their hearts and minds bubbled with joy. A feast of thanksgiving would be one way of observing their deliverance from annihilation as a community and possibly death at the hands of the Communists. Still, money was almost nonexistent and the sisters were limited to a diet of rice and once in a while some fish. The feast seemed to be something that would be a long time in coming about. Whereupon a parishioner stepped in. He showed up one morning with a duck, vegetables and bananas. That would be the feast. The sisters sang and chattered away all morning as they prepared the dinner. The rich aromas filled the house and quivered their nostrils. Just as the meal was put on the table, there was a knock at the front door. Everybody scurried to find out who it was. By the time the visitor had left and they returned to the dining room, the table was bare. Thieves had come through the back door and made off with every bit of food.

Hsinchu was understandably only a stop-gap arrangement in re-establishing a firm base for the community. Bishop Niu and the sisters knew that its growth was paralyzed until proper mother house facilities could be provided for aspirants, postulants and novices. Still, there was that forever-nagging problem of money. Until enough was available, the sisters would have to stay on at Hsinchu, except for those assigned to parish duties near Chung-li, between Hsinchu and Taipei, and Touliu in West Central Taiwan. This arrangement continued until the spring of 1954 when a mother house finally was completed at Mei-shan.

"I met the sisters in Touliu," Father Sun, the parish

priest at Mei-shan, recalled. "There were eight who were assigned to Mei-shan. They did not have much in the way of worldly goods. Just some clothing and a little bit of furniture, mostly beds. We loaded their belongings onto a truck. The sisters then get on the truck, too, and we drove to their new home."

The sisters were delighted. "It was beautiful," Mother Philomena said. "It was the first place we could really call our own permanent home since we had left Shantung nearly seven years before."

At the time, there was no church building. Father Sun conducted services in the living room of a parishioner's house in the town. He built a church—an off-white brick structure—in 1958 close by the mother house. The sisters themselves helped with the construction as a means of keeping labor costs down. They unloaded truckloads of bricks and carried them to the workmen on scaffolds. They helped mix and carry the mortar.

Thus, when I arrived, a year later, there was a brand new church, but the mother house was beginning to show signs of wear and tear because of the harsh weather. Typhoons and earthquakes had already taken their toll of the mud and bamboo buildings. As living quarters go, the convent was undesirable by American standards. Yet, here in the heart of Taiwan, it was a fairly substantial place as against the hovels of some of the low-income Taiwanese. Fundamentally, though, it was a place for the Sisters to begin rebuilding in numerical strength and vocations for a brighter future.

Yet, it seemed they were destined to suffer even more. Summer floods had destroyed tens of thousands of acres of crops, thousands of bushels of fruit, and thousands of fowl and pigs in this part of Taiwan. The area's economy was severely hurt. The last of the floods, in the summer of 1959, gave no warning at all. Sudden, torrential rains in the mountains sent billions of gallons of water and huge boulders cascading like battering rams through the valleys. Steel and concrete bridges were twisted off their foundations. Roads disappeared. Homes vanished and scores of people died. It was a flash flood of almost unprecedented proportions in their area. When the water subsided, huge, flat seas of mud, broken only by thousands of protruding boulders, covered the rich farmland. The sisters' own vegetable garden, which was both a source of income and food for their table, did not escape destruction either. The sisters were back on a very meager diet. In fact, everybody suffered throughout the area because the end result of that flood was a general shortage of food, rising prices and pork rationing. It was no wonder that so much poverty and hunger were evident on my arrival. About the only constructive thing that could be said was that the sisters did have a home they could call their own, that their days of aimless, tortuous wandering had come to an end.

CHAPTER FIVE

My first spring at Mei-shan came early, by late January. The days turned warm and the night mountain air lost some of its nippiness. This change was most welcome. It acted like an elixir, and the touch of melancholy in the post-Christmas holiday period was quickly forgotten. This does not mean, of course, that every day went smoothly. There were a lot of things I missed from back home. One, of course, was a drugstore soda fountain to satiate that awful yearning for chocolate and ice cream. There was no radio at the convent, and the only music available was the strange-to-the-ears, sing-song, wailing Chinese opera and native songs that floated on the wind from extra-loud radios down the street. Loud radios, incidentally, were something I had to get used to. Many Chinese do not keep theirs low, which is something of an enigma since the Chinese themselves are not a loud, boisterous people. There were no American or European movies in the town. If there had been, I could not have gone. Under Chinese custom, honorable girls and women do not go unescorted to the theater or other entertainment media at night.

Still, I had plenty to keep busy, and adjusted to the missionary-convent life. My days were crowded. There were now more house calls that meant walking as much as ten miles up and down rutty, narrow, water-buffalo cart roads that serviced the bamboo cutters and banana and sugar cane farmers back in the mountains. In rainy weather, the roads were gummy, slippery and ankle-deep in water. In the dry season, they were panhard and dusty. When not making house calls, there was work at the clinic. There were also the daily language lessons under Sister Raphael Chan's tutelage, from four to ten hours a day, depending on the medical caseload. Actually, the days were never long enough, and I was worn out by the time I fell in bed around eleven o'clock at night, sometimes midnight, after trying to write some letters to the family and friends before retiring. On the other hand, I, as a layman, was more fortunate than the sisters and novices. Their day began at 4:45 A.M. I could sleep longer, or just in time to scramble out for the six o'clock mass.

In this period, there was a break in the medical routine that permitted me to obtain a close look at Chinese psychology and philosophy through parts of their culture. It came about with the Chinese New Year—Lunar 4658, the Year of the Rat. Naturally, as a Westerner, I did not fully understand the importance of this celebration to the Orientals. Through my still-feeble Chinese, I picked up a word here and a phrase there about the forthcoming New Year, pieced them together and immediately discounted what I had deduced, namely, the observance went on for two weeks. Nothing, no matter how important, I told myself, could go on that long! The father of a patient was the first to really awaken me about this facet of Chinese life. Out of it came two facts. One, sickness can be real, but because of beliefs rooted in thousands of years of practice, it "does not exist" during the New Year season: a person seeing a doctor will be "sick" until the next New Year. Two, it is sheer futility to try to change the viewpoint of the people when they are convinced they are right. They might even agree, out of innate courtesy, that you have a valid argument, but change is difficult because beliefs are firmly entrenched in customs and legends that pre-date the birth of Christ. Therefore, any change must come gradually and not just overnight.

Extensive reading about China and the Chinese through the years had forearmed me about the Chinese way of life. Yet, the first-hand introduction to some of these aspects did not come about until one day in the midst of a language lesson. A sister brought word that a man and his daughter were at the gate and wanted to see the "American doctor." They had come by bus from a town about twenty miles away, a place I had neither visited nor heard about. The father had heard about me, though, through an always buzzing grapevine that continues to amaze me, even to this day.

"Who told you there was an American doctor here?" I asked as we walked into the clinic outside the brick-walled compound.

He seemed surprised at my question. "My wife," he finally said, and hurried on to explain that his daughter, who was sixteen years old, had been ailing since she was five. "I have spent much money, but nobody can seem to help her. She cannot eat or drink unless somebody helps her because her hands shake too much."

I nodded as he talked, but, at the same time, I was thinking of something else in his connection. "How did your wife hear about us?" I asked out of curiosity. The grapevine had been sending us more and more patients lately, and I was interested in trying to find out something about it.

It is rare that the Chinese drop their politeness and show annoyance. This was one of those few times. "My wife is not sick," he said. His voice was edgy. "My wife is in the best of health. My daughter is sick."

Somehow, but not surprisingly so, something had gone wrong in our communicating. I wanted to say, "I did not say your wife is sick. I said, how did she hear about the doctor story?" But I remembered that awful experience with the garbled translation at the dock in Keelung and decided it would be far wiser to get on with the daughter, whose name was Mah-lan, and her illness.

Mah-lan was a slightly built girl, about five feet, one inch tall. Her face was beautiful in its cameo-oval shape. It was a tawny and unblemished creamy satin, so typical of all Chinese whose skin is among the most beautiful in the world, if not the most exquisite. Her head was bent forward slightly and her hands folded below her stomach. She stood silently behind her father and made no effort to join in the conversation. This obeisance was, of course, natural among the Chinese. The father speaks for the family. I listened closely while he explained again about his daughter's inability to raise anything to her mouth without help.

After his description of the onslaught of the ailment and its effects, followed by my examination of Mah-lan, I was satisfied that its form paralleled Parkinson's disease. Fortunately, there was some medication in the clinic. It had come as part of a shipment of physicians' samples that somebody collected back in the United States and sent to Mei-shan. I gave the father enough for a week and asked him to bring his daughter back for another examination at that time.

"One week from today?" The father frowned.

"Yes."

"That is impossible."

"Why is it impossible?"

"It is the New Year."

"Oh, all right," I said. "Come back the day after that—a week from tomorrow."

He shook his head, closed his eyes and sighed as though to say, "How stupid can you be, woman!" When he spoke, his tone was that of a father talking to a child. "I do not think you understand what I am saying. It is the New Year. I will come back after the Lantern Festival."

That observance was three weeks away, signaling the end of the Chinese New Year season. He was adamant and there was no use trying to change his mind. He kept his word, though, and after a few months of treatment his daughter responded beautifully. Mah-lan was able to lift things without more than a trace of shakiness. Later, she went to Taipei and took a position as a clerk in a business house. The day I started my novitiate she came from Taipei with a huge bouquet to join in the festivities. Word had reached her through the grapevine.

Meanwhile, I still could not rationalize that the Chinese New Year would last two weeks even though the sisters tried awfully hard to make me understand. I believed it would be pretty much of a one-day affair, like the Gregorian Calendar New Year celebration back home, and would quickly peter out with a few parties now and then. I was dead wrong. The clinic did no business at all; nobody would flirt with being "sick" for a whole year. There was not even an emergency out in the mountains.

I also found out that the New Year is the biggest, noisiest and gayest of all Chinese celebrations. Debts are cleared up to start the year with a clean slate. Everybody gets new clothing. Even the poorest of the poor manage to buy or make one set of clothes. In a way, the clothing part of the festivities was remindful of Americans' shopping sprees for Easter finery. Sewing and shopping start at least a month before the New Year. Lavish dishes are prepared, starting weeks in advance. There are such delicacies as *nien-kao*, made from rice flour, water, sugar and banana oil, simmered for nearly a day into a thick mass that is then put into dishes to dry out; *ch'ung-tzu*, rice and peanuts wrapped in bamboo leaves and steamed; *chiao-tzu*, that ravioli-like food filled with ground pork, vegetables, garlic and salt and then steamed. There are roast duck, sweet and sour pork, bite-size pieces of breaded pork crisply deep-fried and served in a tangy sauce; and succulent prawns glazed in a sweet and sour sauce. There are watermelon seeds, peanuts, cookies and candies. The tables seem ready to crumble under the weight of all the mouth-watering foods. One table is set aside for the gods, and quite frequently it is put in front of the house. What is offered to the gods by day is eaten by the family and visiting relatives at day's end. The fact that the food sits out in the hot sun all day can have some nasty after effects, namely, diarrhea. Still, the Chinese do not seem to mind. And even a serious case of it won't send them off to a doctor for relief. After all, who wants to be sick for a year?

The Chinese New Year arrives with an ear-splitting explosion of firecrackers that goes on and on and on. Businesses close down. Families visit with relatives and take long trips to historic spots and public parks. Mei-shan is one of the big tourist attractions at the New Year. It has a small zoo and, of course, plum blossoms that draw visitors by the thousands. The Chinese love beauty and Mei-shan is one of the lovliest of scads of scenic places that abound on the island. If the New Year falls early, in January, before the trees start to bloom, artificial blossoms are displayed. Photographers come armed for this possibility and do a land office business. Who can tell a real from an artificial plum blossom on a photograph? If the New Year falls late, in February, the sub-tropical weather has already turned warm and the trees are in full blossom. (The Chinese use the lunar calendar for their festivals and the New Year can come anytime between January 21 and February 21.)

The plum blossoms were just beginning to burst from their green buds for my first Chinese New Year at Mei-shan. There was a holiday excitement as the visitors poured in by bus, car, taxi, bicycle, motor scooter, on foot and even by water-buffalo cart. The town hall square, more than an acre of land in sort of a half-moon shape, swarmed with laughing, eager crowds. Brightly-colored cloth "dragons" of red, blue, green, orange and yellow—carried by men and boys—curled and danced ferociously. All the while, thousands of booming firecrackers created an awful din. Their acrid blue smoke joined with the pungent gray and brown smoke from imitation paper money being burned outside the one-story stores and homes. There seemed to be dozens of these ceremonies going on all at one time. But they all had one basic meaning: rout evil spirits and bring good fortune. I kicked myself for not having a camera. Here was a photographer's paradise—everybody so exuberant and everything so colorful. This was still another face of China and the Chinese I was so rapidly growing fond of, the belly-deep laughter and the gay dances bubbling out from underneath the somber dignity that is ever-present in their work-a-day lives.

The New Year gave all of us at the Our Lady of China community a chance to catch our breath. The kindergartens, conducted by some of the sisters, closed down, as customary. There was, as I noted before, nothing doing at the clinic. Things slowed to such a leisurely pace inside our compound that it felt like a vacation. Well, not quite. There was our large vegetable garden to be tended, the chickens and pigs to be fed and watered, eggs to be gathered, clothing to be mended, crochet work and the making of vestments—all forms of raising money for the community's support. The two weeks went by and the New Year observance closed with the Lantern Festival, which had its origin scores of centuries ago in the belief that by lighting torches the Chinese could find the heavenly spirits as they floated around in the first full moon's light. From then on, the tempo picked up and the days raced into weeks, the weeks into months.

There were still many annoying, even frustrating inconveniences, to be sure. Public transportation was by overcrowded bus, the sort that looked like the rural school buses of the 1930's in the United States. They were built to carry about forty children, but around Mei-shan were often sardine-packed with loads of as many as sixty grownups. A trip usually meant a splitting headache. The mosquitoes were another bothersome and painful problem. The lack of a Western-style bathroom was something I could not completely adjust to—the out-of-the-bucket "shower" and outhouse. Many of my sleeping dreams were centered on luxuriating in a real bathroom. And then there were the snakes, some deadly poisonous and some harmless. All the sisters went to great pains to play down their existence in a sincere effort to keep me from being frightened.

I had been at Mei-shan about four months before encountering one for the first time. It scared the daylights out of me as I stepped into the showerhouse, a cubicle sort of a building tucked away in one corner of the compound. Its body, less than three feet away, flashed into a coil while its head and neck rose up and tongue danced wildly from its mouth. It looked like a python or cobra such as snake charmers use. For a moment, I was frozen rigid. Finally, I let out a scream and raced into the middle of the yard, hollering, "Snake! Snake!!" Sisters hurried from the three buildings bordering the yard. Father Sun, who was conducting a class in theology, ran up. There was great babbling all around, and I just kept on screaming, "Snake!" and pointing to the showerhouse. Father Sun killed the thing, but by the time he had finished the job the snake was so squashed it was impossible to tell from its head what it had actually looked like in live form—diamond shaped, the poisonous variety, or the nonpoisonous oval shape. Overall, it measured six and a half feet. Later, I visited the snake department of the U. S. Naval Hospital in Taipei, but nothing among the specimens common to Taiwan resembled it.

A bowl of hot tea and some good-natured joshing calmed my nerves, and pretty soon I was laughing, too, about the whole affair.

"You have been properly initiated to life at Mei-shan—mosquitoes, red ants and now a snake," Sister Raphael joked. "Do you think you will stay for a while?" She laughed some more. It was the largest snake the sisters had seen at Mei-shan, and they thought it funny that I should find it when I feared snakes the most.

Life takes many strange turns. The snake incident brought me closer to the sisters than ever. When Sister Raphael used the expression, "properly initiated," it contained a tremendous amount of truth. From the day I had arrived all of us had established a warm rapport. Yet, I had a feeling of not quite belonging—a part of convent life, yes, but still not quite "one of the girls," so to speak. The snakes, for instance. All the sisters knew about them, but they did not want me to know. I was the first Western lay missionary in their community. They wanted to protect me from as many hardships as possible under the erroneous belief that in the United States life is easy, life is comfortable, life is beautiful—no worries, no complications, no poverty, no hunger, and perhaps not even snakes. When the snake episode was over with it seemed that a big concern had been lifted and everybody gave a great big sigh of relief. Now, all of a sudden, sitting there sipping our tea and laughing as some of the sisters related how horrified they were at the sight of a snake, there was a feeling that I really belonged in the community. Any vestiges that nuns are "different" from laymen—an unassailable group of black-gowned automatons, in a sense—disappeared that day. They, too, had fears. Thus the only real difference was in a theological sense: they had dedicated their lives solely to God, working together as a community.

I relished the atmosphere of being a part of this big family. All my childhood and teens had been spent in solid family surroundings. My parents and their brothers and sisters all lived close to each other, either in small cities or on nearby farms in Illinois. They visited back and forth frequently. Christmas, Easter, Memorial Day, Fourth of July, Labor Day were big family get-together days. In all the homes, the close-knit ties of family life were paramount. Maybe it was this family togetherness that I found at Mei-shan that made me feel so much at home. Additionally, nearly all my life was spent on dreams and plans of going to China and becoming part of Chinese life. I had accomplished that much, at least, as a lay missionary with the Our Lady of China community. Still, I was not satisfied. I had found the rainbow, but where was the pot of gold? Was it here at Mei-shan and had I missed seeing it? I was rapidly approaching my twenty-eighth birthday and many questions began to hound me. What was my purpose in life? Did my life really have a purpose as it was now being lived? When my two-year commitment to the community was over in the fall of 1961, I would be twenty-nine years old. What then? Stay here at Mei-shan, or drift to another place in the Orient, stay for a while, and then drift some more? And most important of all—how could I best serve God and His people?

There were plenty of opportunities to go elsewhere with worldwide public and private health groups and work in my profession. In fact, such a change had been suggested in letters from friends in the States. I carefully weighed all the suggestions. Some, including one job offer, sounded tempting. Yet, each had a drawback: the lack of spiritual purpose. I mean simply that treating the sick, while an honorable and very important vocation, was not enough for me. There had to be a deeper purpose, rooted in the laws of the Church, of saving one's soul, spreading the Word of God to the people who never had the opportunity of knowing the true God, and being a witness to Christianity so that non-Christians can see Christian love at work through freely given charity. For charity is love. No, I did not think of using the clinic or the sickbed as a pulpit to win converts before handing out medication. Such a practice was, in my eyes, revolting. It still is and I do not tolerate it in our clinics. In fact, that is a strict rule of our community, too. No "rice bowl" Christians—that is, giving only to those who are willing to adopt Christianity in exchange for a handout, only to find them going back to their original beliefs when the giving stops.

I began rereading Father Lebbe's biography and pondered his problems as against mine. Father Lebbe had seemingly insurmountable woes that piled on top of each other from the day he landed in China in 1901 to his death in 1940. He had enemies who worked feverishly to embarrass him, to have him removed from China, and even demanded that he be defrocked. Yet, he cheerfully and determinedly went about his work of being a witness of Christ. I asked myself, what are my problems? Mosquito bites, snakes, inadequate transportation for sick calls, long hours of work, lack of medication and inadequate hospital facilities but potentially thousands of patients in need of medical help. A mud and bamboo home with a ceiling that leaked and a floor that was constantly wet from moisture seeping up through the cement from the ever-damp earth. No soda fountains, movies or radios. When I measured my problems against Father Lebbe's, I was in clover.

In his biography were stories of the two European women, each from affluent homes, who went to China in the 1930's and joined his Little Sisters of St. Teresa as Sisters Luke and Chow. They went through hardships that paled mine.

I will mention one of theirs, for it is sufficient to illustrate the point. Their beds were platformed earthen floors; their pillows were bricks. I had a wooden bed, a mattress and soft pillow, and a mosquito netting over the bed.

I told myself that if Father Lebbe and Sisters Luke and Chow could put up with such burdensome problems and hardships, so could I, since mine were relatively insignificant.

My mind dwelled, too, on Mother Paul Ketter, my Latin tutor at St. Teresa's Academy in Decatur. She had been a lay educator before she joined the Ursuline Sisters when she was about forty years old. She also had sought a life that would fill a void and found it in her middle years. She was not just a great person in her understanding of her fellow man, she was also one of the happiest people I had ever met. She had peace of mind. I recalled laughing inwardly when she said I would become a nun someday. Now, I was not taking her forecast lightly, since I had begun considering my vocation in the light of a lay missionary versus that of a nun. True, as a layman I could be a witness of Christ. Yet, there seemed to be an invisible wall that withstood a layman's efforts to devote himself completely and without reservations whatsoever to the work of God and the teachings of Christ. It seemed that full and thorough devotion, as a witness, could come only by getting around the barrier and into the world of the religious. Was I prepared to do this? Or better still, was I capable of exchanging the freedom of a layman for the cloistered, confining, dedicated life of a nun in order to give myself completely to God?

When I arrived at Mei-shan, dead tired and spiritless, I called on God to give me the strength to last six months before deciding whether to go back home or stay on for two years. The six months were up. I reviewed them carefully. Had I made any contributions to the people's health?

Yes. Had I adjusted to the culture of the Orient? In part, yes. Did I still get a warm surge when I thought of being with the Chinese? Yes. Were the sisters in the Our Lady of China community cheerful and stable, and did they permeate joy in their religious lives? Yes. Did they appeal to me as life-long companions in the close confinement of convent life? Yes. Did they like me? I believed the answer would be yes. Would my life be fuller if they would let me become one of them? I weighed that question against another: would I accomplish as much in bringing peace of mind to myself and being a witness of Christ if I were to remain at Mei-shan as a lay medical missionary? The answer to the last question was no. I felt my purpose in life was to become a nun with the Sisters of Our Lady of China.

I picked a Sunday afternoon, the quietest period of the week, to talk over the decision with Father Sun and Mother Philomena. It was mid-June and the weather, compounded by the extreme humidity of our sub-tropical area, was boiling hot. I wanted to look my best for this occasion and tried on different dresses, all of them bought more than seven months before in the States as I prepared for the trip to Taiwan. None fitted very well, because it had been months since the sisters had attended to them, and I had gained still more weight. The poor fit of the dresses was something I had known, but had sloughed off as unimportant. After all, sick people are not interested in somebody else's clothing even when it is a bit snug here and there. Now the sartorial facts of life hit home at a time when I wanted to look my best. One dress, a light cotton print, was a bit roomier than the others. I squeezed into it (with a vow to go on a diet), went across the compound yard and knocked on Mother Philomena's screen door.

"Mother Philomena, please come with me to see Father Sun," I said. "There is something to talk over with both of you." Father would naturally have to be in on my plans. Also, he would act as translator since he spoke some English and I did not as yet trust my fluency in Chinese to go over the decision first and alone with Mother Philomena.

She nodded slightly, but did not move from her desk. Her eyes had a concerned look. It was at this time that a disease had decimated our flock of around fifty chickens practically overnight. That was a terrible blow; the chickens were both a source of food and income. Now we were down to five chickens, the prospect of losing them, plus the worry that if already low funds were used to buy more chickens they, too, might die almost immediately by picking up the disease that had raced through this flock. Somebody once said that money is the root of all evil. He could have added that lack of money is the root of worry and heartache. Mother Philomena, as our superior general, knew that better than most people. These were extremely trying times for her.

"Did you understand, Mother?"

"Yes—yes, Gloria. All right, we will see Father Sun."

Mother stands five feet, four inches, and, although she is in her forties, she has the straight carriage and litheness of movement of a young student. But now, as she stood up, there was a slight stoop in her shoulders. Her face, which could vie with any of the teen-age soap-ad girls in the States for clarity and firmness of skin, was drawn and faint lines showed in her forehead and around her mouth. Obviously, her worries hung heavily.

We cut across the yard, in full and riotous bloom from many varieties of flowers, went through the compound gate, turned abruptly into the churchyard and into Father Sun's quarters. Mother spoke briefly but rapidly, much too rapidly for me to catch the words.

"What is it you wish to talk about?" Father Sun asked. He seemed bothered by something, too.

I foolishly thought it better to start from the beginning to illustrate the evolution of my thinking about joining the community in a religious role.

"When I came here nearly seven months ago," I began, "everything was so different than at home. I was not quite sure whether I would like it and, with the help of prayer, made a compact to withhold a decision for six months on whether to stay or go back home."

After that deliberately composed introduction to the main theme, I quickly sketched out—no doubt too quickly and sketchily—the path my thoughts had taken in coming to the decision to seek admittance to the Sisters of Our Lady of China, and closed on this note:

"There are still a few patients who have been under long-term care, but they can be discharged in about a month. Will it be all right to start, let us say, a month from now?"

Father Sun listened courteously and without expression of any sort. Then he translated and tears came up in Mother Philomena's eyes. After the translation mix-up between her and myself at the dock in Keelung, I should have been immediately suspicious, but was not. She is overwhelmed with happiness, I thought. And I was happy, too, not so much that they would accept an Occidental—the only one in the community's history, or, for that matter, the only North or Latin American in any all-Chinese community—but that Mother herself was pleased with the decision.

She said something in Chinese that I could not understand. Father Sun translated it.

"Mother Philomena said she is sorry," he said. "I am sorry, too. We did not think you had such a thing in mind. We are sorry—both of us are very sorry."

My heart sank right down to the soles of my feet. I was being rejected and wanted to ask why, but Father Sun went on.

"We know that many facilities, such as the bathroom, do not meet Western standards. We regret that very much. We have all come to think very highly of you and your work. We deeply appreciate what you have come here to do. Again, I must say that we are sorry that you are not happy and are leaving in a month. . . ."

"Leaving in a month?" I broke in, completely forgetting my manners. In the States, people have gotten into a bad habit of interrupting. Such discourtesy does not exist among the Chinese. They wait until a speaker is finished. I wanted to bite my tongue out for this breach, but, at the same time, I was too downhearted and upset to think properly. "What are you talking about?"

"Your decision, of course."

I looked at Mother Philomena. Her head was bent downward. I turned back to Father Sun. "I think there is some sort of misunderstanding."

"No, do not think that way. We understand how you feel. Life here is different. The food is different. The customs are different. Our living conditions are not fully adequate, but that is only because the sisters do not have the money as yet to build a better convent. We should not have let you come in the first place until we were better prepared to provide some of the comforts that are very important to the people in the West. Please accept our apologies for the many inconveniences you have had to go through."

I did not know what he was talking about. Furthermore, I frankly did not know where to begin to get this mess untangled. And then a thought wildly entered my mind. Was this the Chinese way of obliquely saying that I was no longer welcome? Unlike Americans, who say what is on their minds and usually let the chips fall where they may, the Chinese are never so direct in matters of reproach or disagreement. They use a delicate, roundabout method that is so subtle that sometimes, in the end, you think it was your idea all along.

"Father Sun," I finally said, "are you suggesting that I leave here?"

It was his turn to be surprised. A hand lifting a cigaret to his lips stopped abruptly in mid-air. "Most certainly not. We would be happy if you remain with us."

"Well, that's what I have been trying to tell you all along," I blurted with a tremendous amount of relief. "I want to stay. I want to become a nun—here, with the sisters."

From that point on, it did not take much doing to get the purpose of the meeting with Mother Philomena and Father Sun squared away. They were happy; I was happy. But they insisted on a two-day retreat before I made a final decision about beginning the postulancy. The retreat started a few weeks later. Immediately after the retreat, I sat down and wrote a letter home. There had been some vaguely worded hints about the direction of my thinking in a few previous letters, and then the fact that I would go on retreat was relayed in the last letter. Now, it was time to tell my family the results.

I wrote, "I made the retreat and it was a very good one, indeed. If you remember, the purpose of the retreat was to determine what I was going to do with my life, and good time that I should decide something since I am not getting any younger. As for working with any of the secular groups we talked about in other letters, I am afraid that sort of vocation leaves me cold. I want something where I can dedicate myself completely to God—doing God's work—and in an organization where there are others closely united (united as in the unity of family) doing God's work—living, praying and working together, a group that cannot be dissolved except in death. Therefore, the life of a sister seems to be the life for me.

"Here I am at Mei-shan—in China which I have loved

many years without really knowing much about it before. Now that I know it from experience more than reading, I love it more than ever. The sisters here have been very kind to me and we have gotten along through seven months with very little discourse. I am still struggling to learn Chinese; it is a difficult language. Also, they want me as one of their sisters. Therefore, why should I go looking elsewhere for a convent when everything here seems to be right. Mei-shan seems to be where I am happy; it also seems to be where God wants me. Therefore, I have decided to enter this community as a postulant and try it out."

CHAPTER SIX

It seemed around the time I was mulling my future that everything started popping at once, most of it good, and ranging from mysterious letters containing U.S. dollars to catching butterflies and collecting postage stamps for sale back in the United States. That was quite an exciting and hope-building period in the community's life. As things turned out, this was the major turning point for the better, although none of us fully realized it when the letters began arriving late in April of 1960. Each one mentioned that the enclosed contribution, usually a dollar or two, was for a new convent and novitiate. That was wonderful! We certainly did need a new house. The leaky-roof, cracked-walls place we called home was a constant reminder to include a larger, water-tight mother house in our daily prayers. But what prompted the letters?

The first clue was a clipping from *The Register* of Denver, Colorado, that one of the readers had sent along. "Fight for Existence in Formosa (Taiwan)—Exiled Sisters in Dire Need," the headline read. The article related the sisters' flight from Communist China, Bishop Niu's efforts to re-establish them at Mei-shan, but now their buildings were reaching such a state of disrepair that a new convent and novitiate were mandatory. The article noted that donations could be sent to either Father Peter A. Kuo at St. Canisius rectory in Chicago, or to Mother Philomena at Mei-shan. There was no by-line on the story; no way at all to tell who wrote it, although we did wonder if Father Kuo—Mother Philomena's childhood playmate who helped the sisters escape—had something to do with it. Still, there had been no word from Father Kuo that he had submitted the story to the newspaper. We also wondered if Sister Catherine Chang, who had finished her studies at Marquette and was doing X-ray work at St. Alexius Hospital in Bismarck, North Dakota, was involved. Again, there had been no reference to the story in her letters.

One day in early June, right after the merry-go-round meeting with Father Sun and Mother Philomena about my hopes of becoming a nun, a letter came from Father Kuo. He included a substantial check and a list of donors who had sent money to him at the rectory. Buried in the letter was a casual reference that he had sent the story to *The Register*. The mystery was over.

The heartaches from the loss of our flock of chickens was considerably eased, and we began making all sorts of plans for the future. Every one of us buzzed with ideas. They centered, naturally, on a new mother house with large rooms, a leakproof roof and bone-dry floors. What would it be like to walk on floors that were not always wet? And get up in the morning and put on shoes, stockings and clothing that were not damp? The arthritic pains would vanish! I was so enthusiastic about this bonanza from the United States that I could see a spanking new building rising up out of the ground—with a Western-style shower included—within a matter of months, maybe a year. Well, it did not happen that fast, but we did break ground less than two years later.

Father Kuo with his pen and America with its heart of gold had given us a nest egg of nearly $3,000 on which to build a new mother house. But how could we use the names of the donors to help us in the future? That is, the keystone on which to build direct contacts with the people in the

United States. Aside from Father Kuo, Catholic Relief Services and Catholic Medical Mission Board, we had no direct personal contacts at that time with Americans. After all, we were a native mission group, organized only twenty years before in China by Chinese for Chinese personnel. If more Americans knew our story, I, as an American, was confident they would pitch in and help us grow so that we could more effectively carry out our work. The excellent response to Father Kuo's article solidified that belief.

A master plan began to evolve. First, each donor's name was entered on a file card for future reference. Second, a thank-you note had to be sent to each person. Third, a Christmas letter about the community's work, along with an appeal for additional funds to help us, should be sent to everybody on the list. Out of those three ideas came still a fourth: contact every bishop in the United States about the community's needs, especially a new convent and novitiate. But how to go about it and when? That needed some more thinking. So, I approached Mother Philomena about only the first three points of the master plan.

"Yes, we must thank everybody who sent us money," she agreed. "But the Christmas letter . . ." She paused and thought for a while. "Our work here is important. That is true. Here in Mei-shan the people all know us. But in America—I do not know. We cannot do anything for the people of America in return for their generosity except remember them in our prayers. If we ask them for more help, they will think we are imposing."

Mother Philomena is very modest, yet proud. She would rather cut her tongue out than ask a stranger for help. I weighed all of the things she said, along with her personality, against my own knowledge of Americans.

"As an American," I said, "I know how Americans feel about giving. If they believe in something, they'll give even though it is to a group of sisters halfway around the world. Look how they responded to Father Kuo's article.

"Furthermore, Americans are used to financial appeals. It's part of their everyday living. Hardly a week goes by without some sort of an appeal arriving in the mail. At Christmas time, all sorts of groups, including communities of nuns and other religious bodies, send out their literature to huge mailing lists. Therefore, we would not be imposing on anybody. We would not be hurting anybody's feelings.

"These people who answered Father Kuo's newspaper article already have heard about us. We are not complete strangers to them. The thank-you note would not be the proper medium to go into details about us and our work, and then ask for more money. But a Christmas letter would be all right for a financial appeal."

Mother Philomena listened carefully, nodding her head once in a while. "I believe you when you say that such things go on all the time in the United States," she said. "Americans are different than Chinese, but I want time to think about the wisdom of asking them for more money in a Christmas letter. A thank-you note, yes, please go ahead with that."

Each note had to be personalized. As I was the only one at Mei-shan who could write English, that was quite a chore since there were in the neighborhood of two hundred donors. I wanted to get as many finished as possible before starting the postulancy in early July. Once that period of my life began, free time would be limited because of the hours of study and meditation, plus the language and medical work. So, a lot of midnight oil was burned. And help, too, from some of the sisters who addressed the envelopes.

One name on the list nagged at me. It was Mother St. Joan of Arc Cronin, an Ursuline Sister. When I had become a Catholic ten years before, Mother Paul Ketter asked what I wanted in the way of a gift. She insisted on giving me something for the occasion. I suggested a medal of St. Joan of Arc, my patron saint. The Joan was from my name, Gloria Joan Watts. Mother Ketter hunted everywhere but could find nothing that suited her.

"I have a friend, Mother St. Joan of Arc Cronin," she said. "I will write to her and see if she can help."

A few weeks later, a beautiful medal arrived from Mother Cronin. Now, a decade later and 10,000 miles away, the name of Mother St. Joan of Arc Cronin appeared again. We had lost contact, and I wondered if it could be the same one responsible for the medal. The thank-you note included an inquiry. A few weeks later, a letter arrived. Yes, she was the same person. How small our world really is!

Around that time, something else also arrived. A small, three-wheel truck stopped in front of our gate. Two men jumped out, unloaded a crate, and lugged it through the compound yard to the outhouse. Out came a second-hand, Western-style commode—flush box and all. Father Sun had done some scrounging.

Right after I became a postulant, Mother Philomena gave me approval to go ahead with mimeographed Christmas letters. They were to become the first of an annual Yuletide series to our friends in the States. I am a very slow writer. I write and rewrite. Moreover, there was only an hour or so a day to do this because there were studies, meditation, housework and other tasks common for a postulant. It seemed as though I spent months composing its two pages of single-spaced typing. The text dealt briefly with the sisters' escape from Communist China, life at Mei-shan and the community's work in Taiwan:

> This area is mostly Buddhist, and the people are very faithful to their religion. Yet, the sisters in the five years they have been here have managed to gain the respect of

the people. They have organized a kindergarten and a dispensary. There are approximately two hundred Catholics in and around Mei-shan.

I would like to tell you a little bit about our dispensary. Most of our patients are poor and cannot afford to see a doctor. Therefore, our sisters must act as doctor and nurse, treating serious as well as minor illnesses the best we can, with the limited supply of medicines our friends have sent us.

Not long ago, a very poor farmer brought us his seven-month-old baby. His wife had recently been very ill with a form of paralysis and we had cared for her. Then she became better and could walk with assistance. Still, she was unable to care adequately for their four children. To complicate matters, the father had to be away from home days at a time looking for work. When I saw the baby, he was so weak he couldn't move his head; his emaciated little body was pitiful to behold. We did all we could but lacked enough powdered milk. The child died, but not before being baptized. His soul, indeed, now has the eternal rest it could never have on this earth.

The scene I have just pictured is one that we Americans cannot picture until we have seen it firsthand. I am filled with joy when we are able to help, yet often saddened when I see children dying from lack of food; lack of care, which can be had in this world, but is beyond our reach. Why is it beyond our reach? Because we do not have the necessary funds.

Once again the Americans came through and we raised $1,000 that went into a fund for the community's work.

Meanwhile, I had a couple of pot-of-gold, get-rich-quick brainstorms: butterflies and stamps. I had read someplace that a priest in South America had built a church from money he raised collecting butterflies and selling them on the South American and United States markets. We had thousands of our own flitting around inside our compound. They were beauties, too. We needed a market, of course. Taiwan was out of the question; it had millions, maybe trillions of butterflies. They were a glut on the market. I wrote to Pop and Jo back in Florida to enlist their aid in selling our catch. Pop had just retired and he and Jo had moved to Largo, Florida, to get away from the bitterly cold winters around Decatur. They wrote back that they would scout around for some butterfly dealers.

We hurried and made nets out of some old cheesecloth, hung them on bamboo poles and went to work. We chased butterflies through the flower beds, the vegetable garden, and the orange, papaya, banana and grapefruit trees. We caught scads, selected the most colorful and largest, and freed the others. Each night, we carefully mounted the day's catch on a huge board and tried to figure out how much they would bring on the U.S. butterfly market. We saw the U.S. dollars rolling in. The word finally came back from Florida. The market was dead.

We hung our butterflies as a decorative wall piece. Pretty soon, though, they started to look awfully ragged. It was not hard to figure out why. Our old friends, the red ants, had gone to work.

Well, maybe the butterfly market was glutted, but not the postage stamp business. Why, there were millions of philatelists in the United States, and all of them eager to get their hands on those colorful beauties the Taiwan postal service issues. Off went another letter to Pop and Jo. They agreed that the postage-stamp collecting business was more promising than butterflies. Off went a batch of new issues. Back came a check that netted $1.60 profit, and also a list of rules on how to buy stamps (such things as plate numbers, blocks, commemoratives and so forth, and all Greek to me) and how to ship them to avoid even the slightest damage. To me, a stamp was a stamp for its own beauty and the fact that the edge might be a little bent did not detract from the overall exquisiteness. The philatelic world had other ideas. I could see that the stamp business would not work out too well. All of the sisters and I were far too busy to afford the time to fuss over all the little details stamp dealers insisted on.

Pop and Jo also wrote that they were sorry the $1.60 net profit was such a little bit. It did sound small to the average American. But, to many Taiwanese in our area, it was two days' wages.

"That $1.60 here is approximately $68NT (National Taiwan)," I wrote to my folks. "Here at Mei-shan we use a little less than $100NT a day to buy food for twenty-three people!"

We made some progress in another direction, however—an electric refrigerator. We had no refrigerator whatsoever, not even an old-fashion ice box. That meant that the cook had to go to the market every day for perishables. More important, it meant that a lot of our medication was lost due to heat and humidity. Medicines were much, much too hard to obtain only to stand by helplessly and watch some of them being ruined. This was particularly true of the gelatine-type capsules. Within a few weeks, they would melt into a gooey mass no matter what precautions we took to keep out the dampness. This loss ran into hundreds of dollars a year. Even more vital than the dollar loss was human life. How many times were we at a loss to help somebody simply because we did not have the right medicine in stock, perhaps medicine that had been destroyed by the heat and dampness. For the lack of a pill, people died.

The refrigerator came about this way. On becoming a novice, I would have to give up worldly goods. That meant money, too. Also, we had heard that an American civilian attached to the U.S. military installation in Chiayi City was going back home and had some household goods to sell. We bought his refrigerator with money I had left from my savings. Although it was for the clinic, the cook managed to cram some of her things into it, too. She considered the refrigerator an invention equal to that of the wheel, since she no longer had to walk down the hill to the market and back up every time she needed perishables.

Meanwhile, the decision about my future, reconfirmed during my postulancy, was not difficult to make. I believed that I would be happiest as a nun. November 30, 1960, was the date set for the mass that would admit the postulants into the novitiate. There were three of us. Prior to our group, there had been nine postulants starting in the fall of 1954, some six months after the sisters had arrived at Mei-shan. Seven of them became nuns. Would all three of us be around to take our first vows in the fall of 1962? As it turned out, two of us did—Sister Mary Liu and I. That meant, incidentally, that the community's growth still was averaging out to slightly more than one nun a year. In reality, the community was practically standing still once age began to set in and the attrition by death started.

Shortly before the BIG DAY arrived at the end of November, I had another go-round with Mother Philomena about my VIP status. A few months before that, she had refused to move me into the same quarters with the other two postulants. That prompted an argument at that time, but Mother won, as usual. Now, all three of us would be novices together and I insisted on giving up my private quarters to live with my companions and also eat the same food. I was still being served eggs at breakfast, plus meat at least once a day. Everybody else had rice and vegetables, and only once in a while a little pork or chicken. I argued that this special treatment was unfair, illogical, contrary to novitiate rules, and so forth. I further pointed to one of the vows, poverty, as part of my argument.

"You do not interpret the word correctly," Mother Philomena said. "Poverty does not necessarily mean being in rags. In our case, the way of life of a nun not owning worldly goods. It does not mean that you have to suffer."

"I understand all that. But how would I suffer? I am not different than the other girls."

"Yes—yes, you are; you are an American."

Oh, no, I thought, not that American theme again. For nearly a year, I had argued and explained that Americans are not something special, that they are human beings like everybody else, that millions and millions of them could not afford meat every day or eggs at breakfast all the time. It never seemed to make an impression on Mother or anybody else, for that matter.

"As an American," she went on, ignoring everything I had ever said on the subject, "you must have meat and eggs every day. The people of the Orient are conditioned to a different diet through thousands of years. As for your room, all Americans are accustomed to having their own private rooms. We are not. Entire families sleep together in one room."

"So do a lot of Americans," I said. "Millions of them."

"Yes, it is true that husbands and wives sleep in one room in your country," she said. "But children have their own rooms. You had your own room didn't you?"

"Yes, but . . ." I gave up. There was no use butting my head against a stone wall any more that day. Mother Philomena had me cornered.

"That is what I thought. We will continue the same arrangements."

This battle was not over by any means, and I had another chance at the subject after the novices' mass on November 30. People had come from all over Taiwan for the ceremony: Bishop Niu from Touliu to preside; more than two score priests from all parts of the diocese; Sister Luke of the Little Sisters of St. Teresa and now in Taipei; two Maryknoll sisters from Miaoli; relatives of other novices; patients and former patients, including Mah-lan, the girl who had had the tremors. There was also a newspaperman from Chiayi City. The reason for his visit was the American joining the all-Chinese community. That was a novelty.

"All my life I had dreamed of going to China and living and working with the Chinese," I told him in an interview. Mother Philomena was with us. So was Sister Raphael Chan, who would be the novice mistress but at this point was helping out with the translation. Although my Chinese had improved considerably, there were still plenty of rough spots.

I turned now to Mother Philomena with the next part of my answer. "I also have wanted to be Chinese among the Chinese. I want nothing more than to have that opportunity."

Sister Raphael's eyes twinkled. She was fully aware of my anti-VIP treatment battle. She quickly, but daintily, lifted a hand to her mouth to hide a big grin. She got the point. Mother Philomena's expression did not change, except for a courtesy nod that said thank you for your warm feelings about us. She got the point, too. It took a lot of doing, a matter of wearing her down, but Mother Philomena finally gave in soon after that and let me live with the other novices—and "eat Chinese."

Bishop Niu had come to Mei-shan the day before the ceremony to present us with our novice habits. He had a bad cold. As the day progressed, he felt worse and by evening was quite sick. During a medical examination, his temperature was 102 degrees and his blood pressure alarmingly over 200. He needed a doctor, but refused to admit that he was a sick man. I urged him to stay in bed a few days and forget presiding at our mass. He would not miss that. Almost immediately afterward, he nearly collapsed and we hurriedly put him to bed and started treatment. In spite of orders to stay in bed, our bishop was up at dawn the next day, as usual, for the six o'clock mass. The mass had barely started when he took a turn for the worse. A few hours later, he was on his way to a hospital in Huwei, where he quickly recuperated and went right back to his arduous schedule. He maintained, and still does, that there was too much work to allow illness to interfere.

Life as a novice had now become one of rules and bells. A bell to get up in the morning, a bell to pray, a bell to eat, a bell to go to bed. These were things that all of a sudden became real. As a layman, I had been aware of them, but they had little personal meaning, for I was not bound by convent rules other than propriety. I was no longer a laywoman.

In all the preparations, including an eight-day retreat, to enter the novitiate, one date was almost forgotten. It was November 27, the first anniversary of my arrival at Mei-shan. That fact really did not strike home until a few days after I had become a novice and life had settled down into the routine and confinement behind the five-foot, red brick walls that surrounded our acre of land. Everything suddenly seemed almost bizarre. A year ago I had been a stranger in a strange land—a stranger who had some trep-idations about nuns, and especially how they could be happy and find life actually fulfilling in their restricted world. Now, here I was training to become one. The roadways of a hu-man being's life seemed awfully strange at that moment. One year before, there were great big questions about what to do with my life. Now, everything was all settled; I knew what I would be doing. A feeling of contentment, of peace, fell over me, albeit a question of how to survive a full year without physical contact with the outside world.

The latter pondering was interrupted almost immediately by a clamoring and pounding on the gate.

"The American doctor," a man half-cried. "I need her. My wife is dying."

It was a question in Mother Philomena's eyes of a novice's

1. Sisters take stroll during recreation period at Mei-shan. Nearly vertical mountain forms backdrop.

2. Sister Mary Paul, in postulant's gown, receives novice's habit from Father Simon Fang, assisted by Father Nicolas Miao, at Mei-shan. Mother Philomena Ly stands near window.

3. Sister Raphael Chan leads the novices to their first Mass at the Our Lady of China Church in Mei-shan. Directly behind her is Sister Helen Chang, followed by Sister Mary Paul.

4. The sisters must grow their own vegetables in order to have enough to eat. These sisters are hoeing a cabbage patch. Huge leaves jutting skyward are from banana trees.

5. All novices must learn English as part of their education. Sister Mary Paul teaches this group.

6. This sister works full-time in making vestments to provide some income for the Our Lady of China community.

7. Father Stanislaus Sun explains Buddhist prophecy to Sister Mary Paul during visit to a temple near Chiayi.

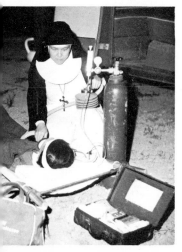

8. Sister Teresa Chung, the pharmacist, administers oxygen to patient.

9. Sister Teresa Chung sets up flow of oxygen for girl patient being transported in the Our Lady of China's ambulance to a nearby hospital.

10. Sister Mary Paul comforts unhappy little boy who had just had an antibiotic shot.

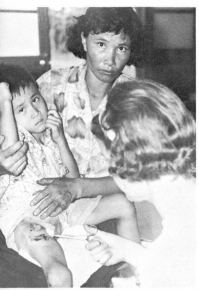

11. Maryann Heim dresses thigh of boy suffering from tuberculosis of the bone.

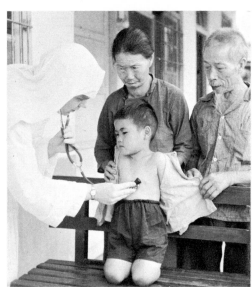

12. Grandparents watch intently while Sister Mary Paul checks over lad at Mei-shan.

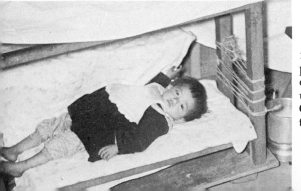

13. This child had double pneumonia. A makeshift croup tent and bed were set up under a table in the Chiayi clinic. He responded to round-the-clock treatment.

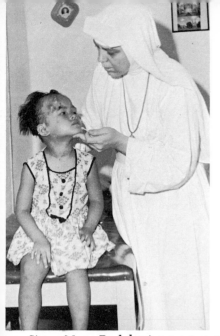

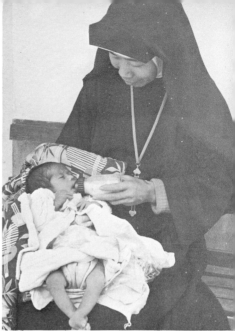

14. Sister Mary Paul begins treatment of severe case of skin infection.

15. Once in a while, somebody brings an unwanted baby to the convent gate. Sister Raphael Chan takes care of this one.

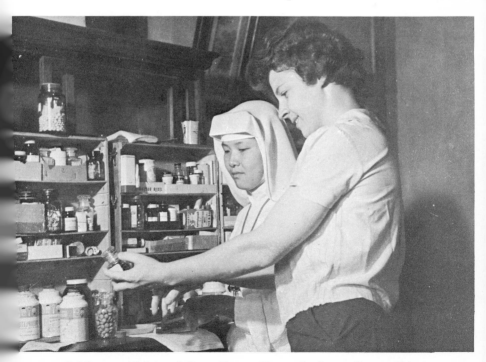

16. Maryann Heim and Sister Teresa Chung check supplies at Chiayi clinic.

17. Mei-shan children gaze in wonderment at Sister Mary Paul reading story about the Our Lady of China community that appeared in the El Paso (Texas) *Times*.

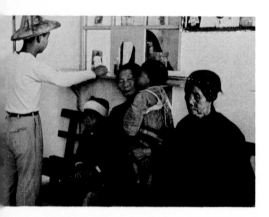

18. The old and young wait their turns at Chiayi clinic while man picks up medicine at pharmacy window.

19. It's lunch time at one of the kindergartens operated by the Our Lady of China community. Food is quite often U.S. surplus provided by Catholic Relief Services-N.C.W.C.

20. Kindergarten girls dance for classmates at school run by the Sisters of Our Lady of China.

21. This is the motherhouse in Chiayi. Generous Americans gave funds for the new motherhouse.

22. Sister Mary Paul gathers eggs in henhouse on the community's property in Chiayi. Chickens are a source of both food and income for the Sisters of Our Lady of China.

23. Mother Philomena Ly and Sister Mary Paul go over the community's hospital plans with Specialist Linney J. O'Malley at U. S. Army and Air Force base near Taipei. Armed forces personnel there contribute to the Our Lady of China's clinic work.

24. Mother Philomena Ly, Sister Mary Paul, C. Edmund Fisher, and Sister Raphael Chan visit his Eminence, Thomas Cardinal Tien, S.V.D., at the Society of the Divine Word's house in Chiayi.

rule being rigidly enforced or humanity being served. She never hesitated.

"Go," she said to me.

The woman's husband, another Sister and I hurried three miles through the mountains to their home. She was in great pain. Her ailment turned out to be a slipped disc that resulted from carrying a heavy bag of rice on their farm. I rigged up a traction device with some old flat irons, the kind that had to be heated on the stove. Word later filtered back that she had returned to work in the fields in a couple of days. The people of Taiwan are truly hardy. I can add that they are proud, ambitious, hard-working and frugal. They are good people.

There were a few other cases—some really dying—that pulled me from the compound during the year. They offered a short break in the humdrum routine of a first-year novice's life. I frankly welcomed those breaks, even though many of them meant long hikes over the rough mountain terrain while lugging an over-sized medical kit crammed with medicines, vitamins (a very big item in treating the malnourished patients), bandages, a stethescope and blood pressure unit. Otherwise, life at Mei-shan was meditation, study and work. There were clothes to be washed, and we did not have washing machines, either hand-operated or electric. We had scrubbing boards, and we heated the water in big vats on the rice-skin fueled brick stove in the kitchen.

And there was the vegetable garden. Most of our sisters and novices had farming backgrounds and green thumbs. I was a city girl with only an occasional childhood visit to relatives' farms in Illinois. I remember riding a cow once and that was about as close to farming as I ever got until Mei-shan. The soil was not my forte, but here at the convent it was a farm-or-go-hungry way of life. Our garden was about three quarters of an acre in back of the convent. Not an inch was wasted. Banana trees lined the inside of the brick wall. Papaya, grapefruit and orange trees were planted in a grove about seventy-five-by-seventy-five feet. The rest of the space was given over to peanuts, which we sold outright, tomatoes, carrots, cabbage, lettuce, onions, sweet and white potatoes and green beans. Because of the climate, we had practically a year-round growing season. That was important, too, as we ate from the garden and sold the extra fruits and vegetables to help supplement our income—to buy rice, flour, sugar, salt, tea, our fuel of rice skins, dry goods to make our habits, and also vestments we sold to priests; and to pay for repairs to the always-in-need-of-repair buildings and for upkeep of some of our sisters assigned to mission stations as kindergarten teachers, religious instructresses and parish workers. Off in a corner of the property was a chicken coop that held sometimes 100 birds. We sold the eggs and once in a while when some of them took sick we would kill the ailing ones for our table. We usually had a pig or two, sometimes three.

All of us did farming chores. Nobody was excused. It was hard, back-breaking work, especially for anybody not used to it. I quickly discovered muscles that even medical science never dreamed about, or else they neglected to include them in the textbooks. Many times, after a day in the garden, I never heard the nine o'clock bell to retire. I was already sound asleep. But the bell to arise at a quarter to five in the morning was a torture gong. Oh, what a good, hot shower would have meant on those muscle-aching mornings!

A rutted, dirt roadway climbed the mountain beside our convent. Near the back of the garden, the road's elevation was higher than the wall. Foot traffic, and once in a while a water-buffalo cart, moved up and down the hill day and night. For the novices, this traffic was our sole contact with the outside world. When our backs would be near the breaking point from hoeing or being down on our hands and knees weeding around the plants, we would straighten up with a few grunts and groans, and rest for a moment. Our eyes would often turn to the road and watch the people going by. Sometimes there would be school children, all of them in the standard khaki clothing of all pupils in Taiwan, hurrying to or from classes. Or there would be a mother, a baby strapped to her back, a wooden bucket hanging from each end of a bamboo pole slung across her shoulders, the buckets heavy with her market shopping in the town. Or men going to and from work in the town or in farmers' fields. The passers-by rarely paid any attention to us; they were too busy with their own thoughts and burdens.

One afternoon, after what had seemed like years of hoeing the cabbage rows, I pulled up, stretched cramped and tired muscles, and leaned on the hoe for a few minutes. Two men coming down the hill stopped and stared. One of them pointed at me.

"Ah, see the rich American *ni-ku* (Buddhist nun)," he said to his companion. "She doesn't have to work." In Buddhist monasteries, the wealthy *ni-ku* are freed from manual labor and can devote all their time to prayers. The man obviously thought I was meditating while watching the others work.

I boiled at his thoughts, even though he was expressing a common belief the world over—an erroneous notion that every American drives a Cadillac, lives in a split-level mansion, has campagne for breakfast, and works only at counting his stocks and bonds when he sacrifices time from dancing, swimming, yachting, golfing, and barbecuing three-inch steaks. I have heard many Americans contending that this misconception stems from U.S. foreign aid. I think the real reasons are (1) failure by our government to drive home the fact, through vigorous and constant publicity programs, that the average American works hard and lives modestly;

and (2) most Americans living or traveling abroad, where their dollars usually buy more, live high and mighty. The rank-and-file native people—the cab drivers, servants, waiters, bell hops and so forth—see this and their magnified tales of American splendor and spending have become gospel. Those were the things I wanted to tell those two men about the "rich" Americans. The seething thoughts were broken by laughter around me. The sisters and other novices working in the garden thought the *ni-ku* appelation was comical. After all, a Buddhist nun has a shiny, shaved head and wears a blouse and pantaloons. Sisters—well, they are covered from head to foot.

"*Ni-ku*," one of the sisters giggled, "what are you doing in that habit?" We all laughed and went back to work.

We had another way of supplementing our income aside from the garden and chickens. It was hogs. At that time we had three. Full-grown and fattened on the sweet potatoes we raised. Each one would bring about $1200NT, or $30 in U.S. currency. Also, when we sold a hog, we always arranged to get some of the pork for our table.

We had a golden opportunity to step up our pork production. A generous neighbor offered to give us five newborn piglets because of some past favors. Mother Philomena was up north for a week at that time and Sister Raphael Chan, our superior local, was in charge. She was not enthusiastic about accepting the litter. The principal reason was that we had no place to keep the piglets. They were so small they might have been crushed by the big hogs in the pen. I finally convinced Sister Raphael that I could handle the job. I rigged up a place in the showerhouse. That, of course, brought some complaints, but all I could see were five grown-up hogs bringing in $6,000NT a few months later. We needed the money. All the sisters agreed that was true, but wasn't there someplace other than the showerhouse? No, because it was January, the nights were cold, and the piglets needed extra special care to keep them from becoming chilled and dying. I put them in a strong carton Catholic Relief Services used to ship powdered milk, strung up an electric light over the top and also a blanket to keep in the heat. I set the alarm for one o'clock every morning to get up and hurry out to the showerhouse and check on the piglets.

Everything went along fine. That is, until Mother Philomena returned. When she found out about the little pigs, she was horrified. In the Old Testament, pig raisers were on the lowest rung of the social ladder. So, too, in Taiwan. And here was this "ritzy" American taking care of pigs.

"No," she said, "you are not a pig raiser."

I pleaded but to no avail.

"No, no," she insisted. "We will have to give them away. They are too small and require too much attention."

During the day, she had a change of heart. The piglets could stay, but she herself would take care of them. That night, she overslept. A tragedy was in the making. The light bulb burned out and the pigs nearly froze. They quickly wasted away. She felt bad; I felt bad. She said she was sorry; I said it was not important. But those little piggies never went to market.

Around that time, it seemed that things were not going well for me. It was about two months after Christmas. The piggies were one item. Popcorn was another. For Christmas, the folks back home shipped a huge box loaded with all sorts of goodies—milk chocolate bars, cookies, nuts, ready-mix ades and popcorn. The sisters had never eaten popcorn. We crowded into the kitchen, got some popping and the sisters went wild over it. Why not grow some? I took a handful of kernels, planted a few rows in the garden, and within two weeks the first shoots popped out of the ground. We were going to have our built-in supply. Well, we were, but a duck hatched some ducklings. (We had added some ducks to our "farm" roster right before that.) By this time, the stalks were about eight inches high. The ducklings, scroungers that they are, saw the juicy, green leaves hanging there and immediately went to work. They stripped the stalks bare. That ended the popcorn farming. I was heartbroken.

After twenty-eight years of freedom of movement, it was difficult to adjust suddenly to living by rules and bells, and knowing that the compound gate was barred for a year, except in a medical emergency. Every novice in every community goes through this emotionally gnawing period. The first few months are not bad because the life is something new and vastly different. There is a feeling of gee whiz! is it really true that I finally made it into the novitiate. After a while the glamor, for want of a better word, quickly wears off. Each new day seems like a repeat of yesterday. The routine never varies: meditation, prayer, study, and work.

Many communities have spacious grounds, with trees and benches and lots of elbow room. The walls are off in a distance, giving the illusion that they are on somebody else's property. Our community was crowded into less than an acre—three buildings for living quarters, an outdoor toilet, a showerhouse, a chicken coop, a pig pen and a garden. The garden, by the way, was off-limits to first-year novices except for specified periods of work. The acre could be walked in less than five minutes, even by going the long way around the walls. The walls themselves were close at hand and they sometimes seemed to move closer, psychologically shrinking our acre to the size of a hemmed-in postage stamp.

It would have been an easy thing for utter boredom to have set in, except for the fact that Mother Philomena was a master at the basic psychology of busy hands, busy minds.

Aside from the prescribed periods of prayer, meditation and study, she always managed to have some constructive chore ready to be processed. There really was no time to become bored. Under such conditions, time did pass quickly.

CHAPTER SEVEN

From the standpoint of sheer natural beauty, Mei-shan is ideal for a convent. The mountains are lovely, breath-takingly so in their thick coverage of rich green from the bamboo trees, interspersed with generous patches of creamy whites of the lilies, fiery reds of the huge poinsettias and gold-yellow and bitter-sweet chocolate brown of the brown-eyed Susans that grow wild and as much as ten feet tall in the rich, loamy soil. There is the restful lullaby from the towering, thick-foliaged bamboos when the wind blows. There is idyllic quiet for meditation. Even today, only a few years after joyfully moving to our new and roomier mother house in Chiayi City, we all get a tugging at our hearts, a deep, longing nostalgia, when we visit Mei-shan. The memories of all the inconveniences have faded.

Realistically, Mei-shan had many physical drawbacks. It was an isolated area; it was inconvenient for travel. We had no transportation other than the rural public buses, most of which meandered around the countryside on local rather than express schedules. This cost dozens of extra hours each week in visiting parishes and clinics that could have been reached more quickly from a centrally located city such as Chiayi. In addition, the mother house was too small and overcrowded. And because of the hilly topography, there was no way to expand the acreage sufficiently to provide enough space to build a new mother house and have enough land left over for future expansion. The buildings were falling apart and with each earthquake (oh, yes, we had those, too; sometimes a tremor or more a week) our blood ran cold. We wondered if this would be the one to tumble down our buildings. As each typhoon season loomed in the late summer, we thought of the violent winds and torrents of rain and how they would further erode the roofs and mud walls. Storms in other parts of the year would send thousands of tons of water cascading down the mountainside. Much of it managed to flow into our compound, damage our vegetable garden, threaten our chickens with drowning, and swirl ominously around the buildings. The cement floors were mostly wet from the ever-present dampness. It also seeped into our muscles and joints, and we ached most of the time. The few dry spots on the floors were constantly dusty and sandy from too much sand and not enough cement to bind the mixture.

There was neither an actual convent nor novitiate *per se*. There was not enough space in any of the three, one-story, forty-foot-long buildings for all the sisters. Some lived in buildings that housed novices. Postulants and aspirants (we rarely had the good fortune to have any of the latter and practically each one left in a short time) had to be integrated, too. All of that, of course, was contrary to the Church's idea of housing professed sisters, novices and candidates, but there was nothing the Sisters of Our Lady of China could do to stay within those precepts.

A community of nuns will wither on the vine if it cannot attract aspirants. We had many serious handicaps in this realm. Our physical property was neither attractive enough nor big enough to house more than a few at a time. High school graduates rarely showed an interest in us, and that meant we had to look to younger girls and educate them first through junior and senior high schools before sending them on to college to prepare for their vocations. At that time, the schools in our area were inadequate to continue aspirants' educations satisfactorily. True, we could have accepted girls without much schooling and let it go at that, but that would have been unrealistic. They would have ended up with a lifetime of gardening, housework, sewing and other unskilled and semi-skilled tasks around the convent. Education is a paramount item for any community to be vigorous and effective. School, parish and hospital administrators, teachers, nurses, medical technicians in laboratory and X-ray work are some of the skilled vocations.

Inasmuch as we had no ways of laying a solid groundwork for vocations, it is no wonder that teen-age girls looked to the affluent communities that offered far better living quarters, a more adequate diet, high-grade educational and training facilities. Those communities were Western-supported. The Sisters of Our Lady of China had no roots in the West, that is, Europe and the Americas. Girls went there, wrote glowing letters to their friends back home and thereby acted as recruiters in a sense. Those communities grew; ours practically stood still. We were really too poor to offer the proper atmosphere to carry on a professional apostolate. So, about all we had to offer was hard work, one sister doing the work of three, an ultra-Spartan life, faith in God and an inadequate education.

Every one of us, from Mother Philomena down to the novices, knew all of those things. Bishop Niu knew them, too, and his heart ached for us. He wanted much better for this community, which he had taken over in its infancy when Cardinal Tien received his Red Hat on the China mainland. He nursed it along through the dreadful, tortuous days of the Communist offensive, the disheartening refugee years on the mainland and in Hong Kong and Macao. He brought the sisters to Taiwan and after a while scraped together enough money to build them a home at Mei-shan to start a new life. Then, it seemed like a permanent home, but as time went on, it became more and more obvious to everybody that it had too many physical drawbacks. On the other hand, there never was enough money in the bishop's funds and too many places where it was desperately needed. A new mother house, which would cost in the neighborhood of $30,000, was out of the question. That was a small fortune, and there was nobody any of us knew who could say, "Here is the money."

We did have the nest egg of nearly $4,000 from Father Kuo's article and the Christmas letter. Still, that was only a drop in the bucket for the building itself. Bishop Niu had money in escrow for the land. A paper manufacturer died and willed some property to the Church. Our bishop set aside the proceeds to buy land if and when sufficient funds were available to construct the new mother house. There were heavy demands on him to use that money for pressing needs, but Bishop Niu steadfastly declined to divert even a dollar.

When the Father Kuo article money and list of donors came in, we thought of ways to enlist the bishops in the United States to our cause. The idea finally jelled: an Easter letter bluntly stating our case. We were poor; we needed help; without America's generous heart our community had a limited future. Begging, yes, but it was necessary. But we all had been doing that to some degree for some time now. So, it was nothing new.

"The Easter letter sounds all right," Mother Philomena told me. Her fears that we would be imposing on Americans had pretty much vanished after the excellent response to the Christmas letters. "It will be all right to write something. I will show it to Father Sun and Bishop Niu. You realize that you cannot write and mail personal letters such as this during the first year of your novitiate. That is the only drawback I can see."

"The rules," I said and shrugged helplessly.

"Yes, the rules. If you know of a way that the letter can be handled without your writing and mailing each one, I can see no harm."

An idea popped up. "You could have a photocopy made and some of the sisters could address the envelopes."

"A photocopy?"

"Yes, the way we handled the Christmas letters. I'll draft the text. After the bishop approves it, you can have a photocopy made and the sisters can do the rest—just as long as the letters reach the bishops by Easter."

Mother Philomena's brows knitted. "Why do you put such stress on Easter? Couldn't it be later, or earlier if the work can be finished in another few weeks?"

I could not help but grin while thinking of an American advertising technique of appealing to the emotions. "Easter, as we all know, is such a glorious and happy event," I said, "the letters will find hearts softer at that time, and brimming with more compassion than ever."

There really was no time to waste. The letter had to be written and rewritten, then approved after more changes. Additionally, my time was very limited. There were many hours of prayer; many classes in ascetic theology, and so forth; plus the usual manual labor chores. Putting the text of the letter together was really a rush job. Then a photocopy had to be made and some 225 envelopes addressed by the sisters and put in the mail in time for the letters to reach the bishops no later than April 1, 1961. Easter Sunday was the following day. All of those things had to be done in less than two months. The deadline was met. We all sat back and prayed and waited, and prayed some more.

Replies began reaching Mei-shan by the end of April. All had checks of varying amounts up to $500. In some cases, the money was provided at the expense of projects in which the donors themselves were vitally concerned. There were two donations that were especially heartwarming because of the circumstances under which they were given. One was from the Our Lady of Providence community and the other from the Most Reverend Maurice Schexnayder. The Sisters of Our Lady of Providence were a new diocesan community founded by the Most Reverend Edward J. McVinney, Bishop of Providence, Rhode Island. As a new group, they needed all the funds they could raise for their own development. Still, they organized a bazaar in our behalf and raised more than $300 for our projected mother house. Bishop Schexnayder's diocese took in an indigent and heavily Negro area in the South. Much of his work consisted of helping the poor Negro families. Although he had urgent uses for money in his own diocese, he felt that we, too, were in dire straits and that there was a spiritual obligation to share with us. He sent along a contribution and has since helped us several times.

In the meantime, Bishop Leopold Brellinger, S.J., (now in Taipei) wrote to Sister Raphael Kuo, a member of his parish on the mainland, suggesting that we get in touch with Richard Cardinal Cushing of Boston about our poverty and need for a mother house. Mother Philomena said I should write this letter. I hestitated, as Cardinal Cushing was at that time engaged in raising a large sum of money for a new Catholic university in Taipei. I did not think he would appreciate being approached by us, another Chinese group, for help. Mother insisted, however, and I wrote to him. Cardinal Cushing replied that he regretfully could not assist us because he was involved with too many projects at that time. I left it at that and did not answer. A week or so later, he wrote another letter that he could not help at present, but would we send Sister Catherine to Boston to talk over the possibilities of doing something in the future?

I could hardly wait until the recreation hour to let out a happy yell, and tell the others at Mei-shan about the good news. "Woweee!" I really did let go and holler it. "Listen to this!" My voice carried to every building. Sisters stuck their heads out doors. Pretty soon we were all gathered in a big circle in the front yard. The sub-tropical sun beat down mercilessly, but not one of us felt its egg-frying heat. We were much too excited for that, and everybody talked excitedly about Cardinal Cushing's letter. Each of the sisters and novices wanted to see it. The fact that, with few exceptions, they could not read English did not matter. They wanted at least to hold this letter, touch it physically, as it could mean God's way of answering their repeated prayers and countless novenas. Tears of joy were in many eyes.

I wrote immediately to Sister Catherine, who was still studying in the United States. She saw Cardinal Cushing and air-mailed news that had us soaring even higher with hope and joy. His Eminence would make every effort to enlist the aid of his friends and said he would try to raise $18,000.

"His Eminence demonstrated a sincere and abiding interest in us and our work," Sister Catherine wrote. "When I was ready to leave, he wrote something on a slip of paper and handed it to me. He said it was a reminder to himself of the pledge he hoped to carry out. If we do not hear from him in a reasonable time, he asked that it be sent to him. His Eminence explained that he received so many requests for aid that he sometimes cannot always remember their disposition."

Sister Catherine also asked that I send Cardinal Cushing a thank-you letter in the name of our Mother General and the community as a whole. His reply plummeted our spirits. He could not help us after all.

There was still another side to our mother house coin, a bright side, and we turned to that for comfort. One year before—in April of 1960—we did not have one cent in our mother house fund. Now, through laymen, bishops, priests and nuns in the United States, it held nearly $10,000, and letters were still coming in from the bishops. We were one-third of the way toward our goal. Somehow, some way it would be reached.

What happened after that was almost too good to believe. Cardinal Cushing wrote that he had erred in his letter. A check arrived in the mail shortly thereafter. It was for $10,000! And with a message that he hoped to be able to send another check in the near future. It came a few weeks later. It was for another $10,000. We were overwhelmed. This could not be true. I think all of us went around pinching ourselves for days on end to make certain that we were not dreaming. We were not. It was all very, very true. We would have our new mother house.

For fourteen years—ever since 1947 when the sisters were uprooted from China's Shantung province and began their flight—the sisters had prayed every day and made repeated novenas for a permanent mother house in which they could begin to grow again. The $30,000 in the fund was like an answer to all their appeals to our Heavenly Father. It was like a miracle, as though God Himself had come down and stood in front of all of us. It was something unbelievable that had happened. It was no wonder that, even in our joy and thanksgiving, we were numb, and we wondered if it all was just a dream.

There had been despair at Mei-shan, an ever-present feeling that it was going to take a miracle to get the community out of the rut. This does not mean that the sisters all sat around wringing their hands and moping. To the contrary. They went about their work and everyday convent chores with diligence and heads high. In their minds and hearts, they knew that God had not forgotten them, and one day, at the proper time, He would give them His answer. But if He would only do something!

They had faith beyond most Westerners'. We, in the States, are more material minded. We are apt to be more depressed when earthquakes, devastating storms, loss of a job and other calamities strike us. The Chinese have a way of quietly accepting those misfortunes and valiantly struggling ahead. You will hear them say in times of stress, "*Man-man-tê.*" Literally, it means wait, or slowly. In other words, don't fret but save your energy for the tasks at hand; things will work out for the better someday. All of the sisters had that philosophy. They knew in their hearts that someday God in His wisdom would set aside provisions for their needs. The generous help from the United States was a tribute, indeed, to their boundless faith and patience. In the relatively short time I had been at Mei-shan, I learned much about the philosophy of life from the sisters, but the greatest lesson of all was faith.

In communications with Americans about our needs for a new home, many of them wondered how we could build a halfway adequate mother house for such a small (but not to us) amount as $30,000. The answer to that was quite simple: labor and materials are cheap in Taiwan. Thus, the ability to build a 125-foot-long, two-story, brick, T-shaped building—with honest-to-goodness showers from a hot water tank heated by wood, and many, many other comforts that did not exist at Mei-shan.

We were confident that the funds for the new mother house would be only the beginning of a burgeoning era for the Sisters of Our Lady of China. There was a vigorous spirit among everybody. You could see it in the glittering, bright eyes of the sisters and other novices. You could see it in the ever-present smiles and hear it in the light banter. After all, this was the spirit and effects of progress, and progress was our keynote. Figures of our growth bear this out. Today, the Our Lady of China community lists thirty professed sisters and nineteen novices, postulants and aspirants, the latter ranging in age from junior through senior high school girls. Those figures can be measured against only fourteen sisters and two novices on my arrival at Meishan in November, 1959. At that time, practically every candidate came from the central part of Taiwan. Now, they are from as far away as Taipei because we have something more to offer than hard work and faith. We can offer, for instance, an excellent education and, with it, professional apostolates.

True, the community's primary need was—and still is, for that matter—money. In helping to obtain it for the mother house, I became only the loudspeaker system for the community. The other sisters provided the incentive since they had the determination, the iron-bound will to progress and a firm belief in God's mercy. And I want to stress this: without Sister Catherine we would never have received the money from his Eminence, Richard Cardinal Cushing. She made the personal contact, which is so very, very important in fund-raising. So, I was only the communicator, sort of a letter-writing bridge linking us with the West. Many Americans figuratively have come across that bridge with generous assistance of all kinds: clothing, blankets, medicines, medical equipment, and, of course, money.

At the moment, I want to mention two whose names will appear from time to time. One is Mrs. Edward P. Wall of Chicago, who got to know about us when Father Kuo was a priest at St. Canisius Church in Chicago at the time he wrote *The Register* article. Mrs. Wall was a member of St. Canisius parish. She began conducting monthly card parties to raise money to buy medicines and supplies for us. When Sister Raphael Chan and I were in the United States last year (1964–65) to obtain funds for our hospital in Chiayi, she was of invaluable help in our work. Mrs. Wall has become our midwestern bulwark.

The other person is Harold Anderson, who is president of the Northwest Trophy Company in Seattle, Washington. He was one of many who sent a contribution as the result of Father's article. He sent us still another check later in 1960, and a questioning note a few months after that.

"Dear Sister: You sent a very nice acknowledgment of a small donation I made last spring, and be assured I am happy that it was for a good cause. I wonder if you received the second small donation. There was no reply from you. Did it ever reach you?"

No, it had not arrived, and I was concerned. Were there other people in the United States whose letters had gone astray? If so, I wondered if they thought the Our Lady of China community was some sort of a fly-by-night group that had hoodwinked Father Kuo, reaped a neat dollar harvest and vanished. If such were the case, our good name, and possibly that of Father Kuo's, too, was in jeopardy. Those people would naturally tell their parish priests, relatives, friends and acquaintances, and pretty soon the word would spread far and wide that the Sisters of Our Lady of China were suspect. I immediately wrote to Mr. Anderson that we had not received his second donation, and I also used the letter to pour out my heart to him.

"You know that we live in a mud and bamboo hut," I wrote. "The money from Father Kuo's article has been wonderful, but it is far, far from enough to build a new mother house. We are planning to send letters to all the bishops in the United States asking them to help. If the response is not good, I really do not know what we are going to do. Our sisters work from early morning into the night. It seems as though the harder everybody works the less we have to show for it. Young girls who should be coming to us because they live in our area are turning to other communities much farther away. Those communities can offer much more than we can. They provide warm and dry living quarters, a good education and any number of vocations. Those communities have support from individuals and groups in Europe and the United States. What I mean is that their mother houses are in the West and they have many Western donors and benefactors they can rely on.

"We do not have anything like that, or anybody like that. We are elated when somebody sends us a few dollars. Until you work in the foreign mission field, it is impossible to grasp the full meaning of how difficult it is for a local community, such as ours, to survive. Yet, the local missionary sisterhoods are among the best qualified in building a solid foundation for the Church. Their members speak the language and local dialects, and know the customs of the country. Also, they are more readily accepted by their own people than are missionaries from abroad. The work of the native-born missionaries is on a charity basis. They must have money to operate, but parishioners are generally few and far from affluent. There are no such things as mission magazines, charity drives and bazaars as in the States. There are not enough Catholics here to support such undertakings. Meanwhile, we must depend on the West for help. But how? Mission organizations are able to send only small donations when appeals are made. This money is never enough. True, our Bishop receives money from Rome, but it must be spread thin because there are so many in need. I do believe there is a solution to the local missionary sisterhoods' plight—a new organization that would be set up in the Church to give direct annual aid to them. This is the simplest and best way to strengthen the local communities."

Fortunately, the poor man had big shoulders and an understanding heart. He wrote back: "I never thought of some of the things in the world that way. Is there something I can do?"

You bet there was! We struck up a correspondence and shortly thereafter Mr. Anderson became our principal pipeline, funneling medical supplies and later funds from his relatives, friends and acquaintances. He started a *Mission Newsletter* that tells of our work and needs. It goes to a small, nationwide mailing list of private citizens. He soon became our mission coordinator in the United States. Material and monies from private funds—other than supplies provided by such genuinely warmhearted and helpful agencies as Catholic Relief Services-N.C.W.C. and Catholic Medical Mission Board—are sent to him, and he, in turn, ships them on to us through Catholic Relief Services and a wonderful U. S. Naval service called Operation Handclasp.

In looking back now on the first year and a half at Mei-shan, I sometimes wonder how so much good could have happened in such a short time. It is as though everything jelled in one relatively short span for both the Sisters of Our Lady of China and me as part of them. All of us at Mei-shan talked frequently and freely of God's bountiful blessings on us. During those times, something that one of the sisters said made a lasting impression: "Are we really worthy of what God is doing for us? How can we begin to show Him and His people our gratitude?"

CHAPTER EIGHT

The summer of 1961 hummed by as the tempo of activities built up at Mei-shan. Mother Philomena, Sister Raphael and some of the other sisters joined Bishop Niu in hunting for a building site for our new mother house. Each jaunt resulted in days of excitedly discussing the pros and cons of what they had seen. We wanted to be in a large city that offered good schools for our aspirants, and also excellent express and local bus service that would take us to a network of medical clinics we planned to open. While all of this activity was going on, four of our sisters were assigned to a new junior high school opened by the diocese in Touliu. Two entered college to become teachers, and two others were assigned to a new mission station in Chungli, near Taipei. We were not any bigger, but we had more work than ever. It was all part of our growing pains.

All of a sudden November arrived and my first year as a novice was over. It was great to walk through that compound gate. And even greater to go back caring for the sick, although this would be on only a part-time basis for one more year. There still was the second-year novitiate to complete. That entailed studies embracing spirituality of the community and the community's rules, why we had certain rules and practical application of each one. We had to know every rule and what each involved before taking our first vows. There were also a few theological courses from which I had been excused since I had taken a theology minor at Marquette. But there was no freedom from manual labor. That continued as usual—gardening, washing clothes and so forth.

By this time I could speak Chinese (Mandarin) with a fair amount of fluency and began picking up the Taiwanese dialect, which was necessary because many of the older people in our area spoke only that. All of this studying, of course, was in preparation for returning to clinic duties. Additionally, Sister Teresa Chan, who was my medical assistant, and I had done considerable studying together in getting ready for our work with the sick. This included going over medical books I had brought along from the United States. That is, I translated the medical terms and explained symptoms of various ailments that I had found to be fairly common in the months as a lay medical missionary. Sister Teresa learned quickly and became an efficient aide. I also learned the Chinese names for drugs, dosages and uses since Sister Teresa would be our pharmacist, and I would have to communicate this data to her.

The end of my novitiate meant, too, that I could begin writing letters again. Some of them were in connection with the new clinics we planned in other cities and towns. We needed medical supplies and in larger amounts. One of the letters went to the Catholic Medical Mission Board in New York about our needs. The Board, a non-profit organization, helps mission clinics throughout the world. I also sent along some pictures showing us in our work. The letters and photos became an illustrated article, "A Place of Refuge," in the C.M.M.B. *Medical Mission News*. We were truly spreading our wings. We felt nine feet tall. I also sent letters to Catholic Relief Services-N.C.W.C., Mrs. Wall and Mr. Anderson about our expansion and supplies we would need for the sharply increased medical caseloads. Under the enlarged scope, we estimated treating up to 300 patients a week.

We built four portable chests, two large and two small, that would be carried around to the mission clinics. These wooden chests had partitions for alcohol to be used in sterilizing, liquid and capsule vitamins, antibiotics in both liquid and solid forms for intramuscular and oral dosages, powdered milk for undernourished infants and children, dysentery medicine, de-worming medicine, blood pressure apparatus, and pocket-size medical textbooks for quick reference. It all amounted to quite a load. The larger cases weighed about fifty pounds when packed, and the smaller ones about half that amount.

We had no trouble locating cities and towns to establish clinics. News of our work at Mei-shan had spread, and we had requests from far and wide. Because we had no other means of transportation than public bus, we decided to limit the radius to thirty miles. At first, we did some experimenting with patients, that is to determine which areas needed us most. Talin, Touliu, Chico, Tzi-tzi Chiao and Hsinkong became clinic sites in addition to Mei-shan. In each city we were under the direction of the local doctor as a matter of protocol and medical ethics.

We rarely had the good fortune of being able to reach any destination on less than two buses. Quite often, three were needed, as was the case with Hsinkong. Each working day started at 6:30 A.M. when we would lug our medical cases through the compound gate, walk three blocks down the hill to the bus stop in Mei-shan. The day would end quite often a few minutes before 9 P.M.—just in time to grab a cold supper and hear the go-to-bed bell. If no classes were scheduled, Sister Teresa and I would spend two to three hours the next day in cleaning out the medical cases and filling them again for another early journey to a clinic. If there were classes, the restocking job had to be done in what little spare time there ever was available.

What was a typical day like? First of all, it was frequently steamy hot. There was always high humidity, ranging at times over ninety per cent even on a sunny day. Quite often the temperature boiled up to near 100 degrees, especially down on the sun-baked plains. This was sub-tropical country, with the Tropic of Cancer going through the outskirts of Chiayi City. We never needed a temperature-humidity index reading, such as is provided by federal weather bureaus in the United States, to let us know that the weather was muggy-hot.

Our day actually began when the rising bell rang at 4:45 A.M. We swung into calisthenics as part of the getting-up routine, made our beds, straightened our rooms, went to mass, made our meditations, said the office in Chinese, and finally had breakfast, which more times than not Sister Teresa and I took on the run. It was now time to carry the medical cases down the hill to catch the 6:50 A.M. bus if we were going to Hsinkong that day.

All right, let's go to Hsinkong. That was a three-bus trip of two hours that we made once a week.

At ten minutes before seven, the inter-city bus stop was crowded with people ready and muscularly able to push their way on. Most of the passengers were conical-hatted farmers going out to the countryside to begin their day's work. The farmers, both men and women, carried hoes, rakes and shovels as primary equipment. Quite frequently they had such added burdens as ducks, geese and chickens. Boarding the bus had all the earmarks of the Great Chase in a Cecil B. DeMille spectacular coming to a milling, growling, crushing, elbowing halt in a dead-end street. It was every man for himself; it was also one of the rare times Chinese failed to show courtesy.

Sister Teresa and I quickly entered the spirit of the Bus

Game. We would pick up those heavy medical cases and swing them gently, ever so gently, against a few shins and scramble onto the bus before the victims had a chance to recover. Once aboard, the Bus Game became a bit rougher. Seats were at stake. Agility paid off, and it is doubtful that there are more agile men anywhere than the Taiwanese farmers. Even with such cumbersome items as tools, fowl and sometimes fish, they managed to wiggle and squirm into the only available seats ahead of the women. I should add that this is part of the pattern of Chinese life: men rule the family; women are to be seen and not heard. The bus—packed so full that the driver sometimes could not close the door—pulled out with a lurch, and off we went, crammed, crushed and gasping for a breath of fresh air. The fragrances coming from the wild life aboard was often ruggedly aromatic.

Phase One of the trip was over a new, smooth, macadam road that curved into Talin some twenty miles away. We had to disembark and wait for Phase Two to begin, the bus to Town X. (I never could remember that town's name, and I imagine that psychiatrists would say the reason was that I completely rejected the place—and for good reasons.) Town X was five miles away, reached via a dirt, rutty, rocky road. The bus, always jam-packed, literally bucked, bounced and pitched the entire way. I, the softy American, usually arrived in Town X with a splitting headache. Sister Teresa, on the other hand, seemed to be used to all this. At least, she never complained. In Town X, we had to carry those medical cases three blocks to still another bus stop and Phase Three, the bus to Hsinkong. We again would have to fight our way aboard and usually stand during the five-mile trip. About the only kind thing that can be said about that ride was that it was over a smooth, macadam road.

By the time we arrived in Hsinkong, we were tired,

sweaty and our clothing a mess. We still had to carry the equipment another two blocks to the clinic. The wonderful lady who set aside the building for our use was ready for us—with a warm, cheery greeting, plus delicious almond cookies and steaming, fragrant tea. The lady was Mrs. Teresa Lin, one of the most gracious and charming women I have ever met. Her late husband was a physician, and she reopened his office in a mud and bamboo building apart from her own house just for our use. She kept it spic and span.

As much as we wanted to, we could not linger in Mrs. Lin's home since there was plenty of work to do. A large knot of patients had started gathering as early as eight o'clock in the morning. By the time we opened the clinic doors, there would be as many as fifty waiting and more on the way: aged men and women, young mothers with a child or two by the hand and a baby strapped on the back, young men and teen-age boys and girls. Each one pushed and jostled and clamored to be first inside the clinic. It was the Bus Game all over again, except that this time, Sister Teresa and I had something to say about the ground rules.

The patients' ailments ran pretty much the gamut of what are common in our part of Taiwan: malnutrition, worm infestation, tuberculosis, diarrhea, arthritis, goiters, trachoma and ulcers. It was always a toss-up whether malnutrition or worm infestation was the number one health problem; they were both directly related.

Before going to Taiwan, I had heard Americans say that the Chinese prefer rice to any other food, and that was why they had malnourishment problems. Such a preference is simply not true. They enjoy meat and fish as much as anybody else, but it is not often they can afford a piece of pork or duck, or chicken, or goose. Beef, by the way, is practically nonexistent except in expensive restaurants and hotels in Taipei and other major cities. Cattle require extensive grazing areas, land Taiwan cannot afford to give up since its economy is based to a great degree on agricultural products. Rice is the cheapest staple they can buy. That is the principal reason it is so popular. The malnutrition-causing diet is, therefore, a simple matter of economics and deep-rooted custom.

To compound the situation, our area in Taiwan—sometimes called the island's bread basket—had been hit by violent, raging floods for three straight years. Thousands upon thousands of acres of rice, vegetables and fruit trees had been destroyed in each of the disasters. After each flood, entire families would be in the fields from before dawn to after dark, feverishly clearing out rocks and even boulders washed down from the mountains. A crop had been lost and they worked like beavers to prepare the soil as quickly as possible for a new crop. Such disasters had their ill effects, too, in the local cities and towns and villages whose people's work-a-day lives were geared to the agricultural economy.

So it was not surprising when we took blood tests at Hsinkong and other farming communities in the area that we found some with a hemoglobin count of around 30 and 40 per cent as against the normal 96 per cent for a man and 86 per cent for a woman in the United States. These people, the farm and town families, were simply undernourished. We supplemented their diet as best we could with vitamins and iron. I cannot say that the thousands of vitamin capsules we gave out each month saved any lives. We did see, however, a marked improvement in the health of our patients.

The other big health problem was worms. The hook, round and pin varieties. Hookworm is quite common around Hsinkong and other farming areas. It is contracted through the soles of the feet. Farmers go barefoot while working in the water-filled rice paddies. The hookworm works its way into the blood stream, then into the lungs and bronchial tubes. The victim coughs up the ova, swallows and it goes down into the stomach, from which it migrates into the intestines, latches on and begins to suck blood. Incidentally, pneumonia from hookworm infestation is not uncommon. We have treated scores of such cases.

Pinworm is also common and can spread like wildfire. Most families—the father, mother and children—sleep on one big pallet. The pinworm crawls from the rectum of an infected member of a family and wriggles into the other sleepers. An entire family can be infested overnight.

The major cause of worms, including the roundworm, is vegetables. Human excrement, from outhouses and so-called "night buckets" by the bedside, is the principal fertilizer and also a rich breeding ground for worms. Farmers dip this fertilizer around the plants. Some of it gets on the plants themselves. The ova are thus prevalent in vegetables. Cooking vegetables until they are soft, which is a common practice in the West, would kill the worms. The Chinese, however, prefer their vegetables semi-cooked. This preference has gone on for centuries, and you simply do not change such long-established eating habits overnight, even though I tried.

"I know what you mean," a patient said in rebuttal. "The pot cooked too long one day. It was cabbage. It was soft, and it did not taste like cabbage any more. We could not eat it."

Another patient said, "You destroy the good health stored in the vegetables." She did have a valid point: semi-raw vegetables do retain more vitamins.

And then there is diarrhea. It is common among children who have not as yet built up enough immunity to the germs lurking in spoiling food. There is no refrigeration of any kind to speak of. In the ever-present heat, food begins to spoil quickly. A watermelon, for instance, may be opened in the morning, and by late afternoon begin to turn. Most Chinese can eat it and never have any bad effects. But an American, or a child, will come down with a case of diarrhea. I have had some personal experience with that, and I do not eat watermelons in the late afternoon any more. Or, for that matter, any kind of food that might have been standing around more than a couple of hours.

We never had problems like that at Mrs. Lin's in Hsinkong. She was a very meticulous person. Our only problem, aside from the public buses, was the mob scene at the clinic doors when Sister Teresa and I arrived. Whereupon, I had a bright idea, a carry-over from American customer-handling ingenuity. I would print numbered slips, pass them out to the patients, and bring them in by numerical order. Presto! No more chaos. It was a grand idea, and hadn't it worked out quite well in the United States? It fell flat on its face in Hsinkong, and not only because some of the patients declined to be first-come, first-served regimented. Some others managed to take the slips home, and quite often a child would take the paper and silently chew on it as he waited in line with the mother. Replacement of the slips meant spending time and money on material. We had neither to spare.

Mrs. Lin always had a delicious dinner waiting for us at noon. Rice, fried green peppers, pork in sweet and sour sauce, or some other type of meat. We were famished. Still, we could not take nearly enough time to sit back and enjoy the culinary masterpieces. There were just too many patients to care for, approximately eighty on an average day.

"You must eat slower or your health will suffer," Mrs. Lin would warn us time and time again. "There have been patients here for many, many years. There will be patients for years to come. A few minutes more at the table will not make any difference."

This was *man-man-tê*—in time.

"We want to see everybody," I explained. "It would not be fair to turn them away."

"You will have to deny some. It is always that way. Each day has only twenty-four hours and not one second more. God gave each of us two hands and twenty-four hours to use them every day. Do not try to outwit God."

Mrs. Lin was right, of course. When we closed the doors before rushing to catch the seven o'clock bus to get us back to the convent by nine o'clock, there were always a few patients pleading, and hands tugging at us, to be taken care of. It was pitiful, but we had to abide by convent rules, too. Mrs. Lin understood our plight and would come to the clinic and help us get away by mollifying the patients. She was a devout Catholic and practiced her religion in many ways. She quietly helped many people in times of need or stress. Sometimes she did it herself; other times through her son, then the governor of Yunlin Province.

"If you do not take care of yourself you will be sick," she cautioned us. "Then other people will suffer, too. The people who need you."

All of that made sense, but it did not rule out the fact that we had plenty of work. As soon as the noon meal was over, we would take an hour or so away from the clinic to go to patients too sick to visit us. We followed this practice at all our other clinics, too. These were the heart cases, the stroke victims, the people bedfast with a host of ailments. As we turned down the street from the clinic, cries went up from the people waiting outside the door.

"Do not leave us—you must not go."

"We will return in an hour," I assured them, but it was not enough. They pleaded with us to stay. Their appeals were heartbreaking, but it was necessary to visit also the bedridden.

One of our first house patients at Hsinkong was an elderly lady who had suffered a stroke. The woman had been a clinic patient for a brief time. She had had high blood pressure. During one of our trips to Hsinkong, Mrs. Lin told us the woman had stopped taking the medicine we had prescribed, suffered the stroke, and another doctor ordered her to bed. She had been in bed three weeks. That length of time was all wrong, as it is difficult by then to re-educate the paralysis. The usual length in bed is a week or so. We finally did get her around to the point where she could walk, but she never did regain the use of her right hand. During this period of care, she became interested in Christianity.

"You are always happy and laughing," she would say. We had not thought about that type of emotion. It just seemed to come naturally as part of our work. Other patients mentioned it from time to time later on, but this patient was the first to call it to our attention.

"Do you want us to put on devil's faces?" Sister Teresa joshed.

"Oh, no—no, not that!" The woman laughed while feigning fright. She turned serious. "You never ask me for money. Why?"

"Do you want to pay us?"

"I would if I had the money."

"We know, and that is the reason we do not charge you anything." Our fee system was based on ability to pay. This patient, like many others, was destitute, and we charged her nothing. If a patient was able to pay, the average charge was twenty-five cents a visit regardless of whether it was a house call or at a clinic. Of course, people we knew who could afford more, the affluent patients, were charged a higher rate, as much as fifty and sixty cents a visit. Rest assured, our clinics were never profit-making ventures! And they never will be.

Our stroke patient looked quietly at us for a while. "You are helping me get well. Other people do not bother with me. Is what you are doing have anything to do with your religion?"

Sister Teresa and I tried to explain the concept of charity within the context of Christianity. The woman was keenly interested and finally asked how she could become a Catholic. We make a practice in our clinic work of being solely witnesses of Christ. We sent word to a parish priest, and he gave her instruction. She was baptized and to this day tells everybody that God alone let her walk again.

Her recovery surely must have impressed her son and daughter-in-law, since word came asking us to visit him, too. He was a very sick man, and had been for nearly a year. He had a kidney infection, a bladder infection, a slipped disc, and a serious vitamin B-12 deficiency. He had been a construction worker, but an injury to his back had put him out of a job. He could no longer do heavy work and tried to make a living, a very poor one indeed, by selling ice cream from a cart. But now he was practically bedridden.

"If you will help me, I will become a Catholic like my mother," he said during our first visit. "More than that. My entire family will become Catholics."

I said nothing, either pro or con, about his promise.

"Yes," his wife said, "my husband cannot work. We are poor. We will be Catholics, too, if you make him well."

I still declined to say anything about conversion. Neither did Sister Teresa offer any comments. We wanted no "rice bowl" Christians. Our primary task was to heal the sick. If a patient was sufficiently convinced that our ministrations and his recovery led him to God, we would notify a priest, but only if the patient requested this.

As the man's condition improved and he was able to return to work, he inquired how he should go about changing his religion. I turned the matter over to a priest. A few weeks later, I heard he had abandoned the whole idea. That was not unusual. It was something I had seen and heard of before and would again from many other patients. But it does provide a sound bit of advice for people planning to go into mission work. If they expect to be thanked, or rewarded in some way, they might as well stay home. True, there are people who appreciate what missionaries do for them, but there are plenty who do not understand.

In some ways, missionary work has a parallel with the story about the man with a violent toothache. He telephoned his dentist and pleaded for an appointment immediately. The pain vanished on the way to the dentist's office and he decided to go to a movie instead. A few weeks later, the two met on the street. The dentist said, "I'm curious. Whatever happened with your tooth?"

"It's fine, Doc. Nothing's wrong with it. The pain went away."

"You should have it looked at just as a matter of precaution."

"Doc, I'm telling you it's okay. So don't bug me. When I need you, I'll call."

A lot of people did need us. If we had worked twenty-four hours a day, seven days a week, we still would have had a backlog of patients. As it was, we spent every minute that could be spared in clinic work, usually three days a week and as much as fifteen hours a day, counting travel time and buses.

Within a few months, I began to have a tired feeling, but attributed it to the awful heat and humidity along with lugging the heavy medical cases on the long bus rides. Long hours of work and short rations of sleep had never bothered me before. After all, I had taken extra college courses as outside work at school, worked while studying at Marquette, and did double hospital duty in Chicago to gather money fast enough for the Taiwan trip. I was always big and strong, and have always subscribed to the theory that work does not hurt anybody.

One of the U. S. Army officers stationed for a while at Chiayi City's military installation was the first to call my attention to the fact that I looked run down. He was Major Keith A. Glasgow (now a lieutenant colonel). He began making the trips to Mei-shan when he heard there was an American girl preparing to become a nun with the all-Chinese community.

"How do you feel?" He said it bluntly.

"Fine, thank you. Lots of work, but that's all right. I thrive on work."

"Uh, huh. When you say you're feeling fine, you're not by any chance using my Think Big philosophy, are you?"

Major Glasgow would hammer home his Think Big idea when I had often talked to him about our problems at Mei-shan. He was like a big brother to all of us and listened patiently while we poured our hearts out to him on money matters mostly.

"Even in the gloomiest, darkest hours, Think Big," he would say. "If you don't Think Big, you'll always be small potatoes. Don't look at one little squirrel, for instance, and see how many nuts he saves for the winter. Look at all the squirrels in the forest. The more squirrels you have working for you, the bigger the harvest. That is one way to Think Big."

I had always agreed with his philosophy, and suppose that is how he used it in chiding me about how I looked. "I'm not a doctor," he said. "But I have an idea a doctor would order a complete check-up in a jiffy." He turned to Sister Raphael. "What do you think?"

"Too much work and not enough rest," Sister Raphael

answered. Mother Philomena was with us and she and Sister Raphael carried on a rapid and brief conversation in Chinese. I could not follow it all, but was annoyed with what words I did understand.

"Mother agrees with me," she told Major Glasgow. "Too much work, not enough sleep and the wrong food."

"Oh, please," I said. "It's not that at all. It's the heat."

In the end, though, I did have a blood test run. The hemoglobin count was down to forty-seven per cent. It should have been eighty-six per cent.

When Mother Philomena heard about that, she quickly put her foot down on my diet. "From now on, you will have meat at least once a day." The tone of her voice let me know she would listen to no arguments.

So, the battle of the "eat Chinese" diet, seemingly won months before, was now lost once again. There would be meat and a supplement of vitamins. I perked up, naturally, in short order.

"You are looking better," Mother Philomena said. The jibe was enough to let me know there would be no more nonsense about eating habits.

Meantime, Major Glasgow's tour of duty in Taiwan was just about over. He was going back to the United States for reassignment. During his good-by visit, he gave us some news.

"I don't know how it's going to work out, but some of the men at the PX are interested in trying to do something for you sisters," he said. "We've talked over some ideas, but let the men take it from there. You'll know in a short time."

A few months later, we received a letter from U.S. service-men stationed outside Taipei that a group would come down to see us and talk over our needs. The best I ever could figure out, even after they had spent a day at Mei-shan, was that a corporal, or sergeant, whose name I regretfully cannot remember, had listened to Major Glasgow talking about us. On his transfer to the Taipei installation, he interested some of the other American military personnel there in making a monthly contribution to our medical work.

They have been wonderful!

Each month, without fail, a check arrives from Charlie Flight, the name used by the group of Air Force personnel. This group also enlisted the Army's officers and men at the installation—Trick Four—to help us. When medication shipments from charitable sources in the United States are delayed in ocean transit, the funds fill the gap through purchases on the local market. The money also goes for X rays and laboratory tests. It helps defray hospital expenses in emergency cases. There are still other ways the servicemen have helped. For instance, in one of the itemized statements we send periodically for the groups' records, we asked them to keep their eyes open for a good, secondhand incubator that could be used for premature babies and as a medicated steam inhalator in croup cases. The servicemen bought a new one as a gift.

Thus, a conversation by Major Glasgow at a PX enlisted more Americans for our cause. This was not the only time he has helped us. Back in the States, he interested editors in stories about us. He also encouraged civilians, military personnel and clergy to work in our behalf.

This ever-readiness of Americans to pitch in for perfect strangers always amazed the sisters. Among the Chinese, only street beggars approach strangers. Otherwise, family is the core of life. When a problem arises, or help is needed, the matter is worked out within the framework of the family —the grandparents, parents, sons and daughters, uncles and aunts, cousins, nephews and nieces. Taking problems to outsiders means loss of family face.

The first contact the sisters had with Americans was

during the flight on the mainland of China. Catholic and Protestant missionaries, at the risk of their own lives, gave them medical attention, food and shelter that renewed their flagging physical strength and enabled them to go on toward freedom. The American Red Cross was on hand with food and clothing on their arrival in Hong Kong. More Americans, absolute faceless strangers, answered Father Kuo's article and my Christmas letter, and later the Easter letter to the Bishops. And then American servicemen in Taiwan, and, after that, still more Americans in the United States. Time and again, while the sisters sat around chatting about current matters or reminiscing about less happy days, they said they owed first their lives to the Americans, and now their progress as a reborn community.

"What next!" one sister exclaimed in stunned surprise over the open-hearted generosity of the Americans rather than in expectation of more of their abundance. I was inclined to agree, and how little did we know there would be many, many more "nexts" flowing from the United States in the months and years ahead.

An ambulance, for example. And how we needed those wheels! And Maryann Heim, a registered nurse from Dubuque, Iowa. Hundreds and hundreds of pounds of medicines to keep our clinics going. A hospital. They were all in the future. I really do not know how we would have reacted if we could have foreseen the largesse. Surely disbelief, at the very least.

CHAPTER NINE

Transportation was, without a doubt, a major headache. We could do one of three things: walk, which was extremely difficult while carrying a heavy medical kit; use public buses, which had limitations; or ride a bicycle, which also posed problems. We took a bus only on long trips to our clinics. There was no service to many of the back-country, mountain homes we visited. A bike was employed only if the trip was over good roads. A good road most of the time meant a dirt affair that was not too rutty or steep. If the road was full of holes and rocks, or just a steep footpath, walking was more practical. After a while, I got to know the countryside well enough to decide whether it would be shanks' mare or a bike. Even so, knowledge of the terrain was no guarantee of a trouble-free mission into the mountains. There were both hidden and unexpected pitfalls.

My worst accident and scare came toward the end of the second year novitiate. We received a message in mid-afternoon that a mother had given birth and immediately suffered a stroke. It was a five-mile trip up and down twisting mountain roads, which themselves ranged from good to mostly poor. The trip on foot—a more practical way in this case considering the condition of the roadways—would have required about two hours. We could do it by bike in about half that time. The seriousness of the case prompted use of the faster means of transportation. Sister

Teresa Chan and I slung our medical kits over the handle-bars and rode off. The bikes had no gear shifts, which meant that we would walk them up the hills and ride down. During the down part, we used brakes a lot to avoid picking up too much speed.

One hill in particular, about a half mile long, had a lot of sharp turns. As we rode down out of the last turn, a hundred yards from the bottom, my brakes gave out. It was as though somebody had jet-propelled the bike. It took off lickety split for the hairpin curve that swung to the left at the foot of the hill. On the outside of the curve was a stream. A one-car width concrete bridge angled off to the right. So, here was this steep road formed by a wide Y at the bottom, a creek and no brakes.

"Oh, dear, what's going to happen!" I hollered with all my might to nobody in particular as by this time I was speeding far ahead of Sister Teresa. I was just plain scared silly.

Then I remembered a trick all kids frequently perform for no earthly reason, except maybe to show off and waste some shoe leather when fooling around on their bikes. Jam the shoes' heels hard into the ground. I did and thought my feet were being ripped off by the dirt and gravel. I quickly pulled up the feet, but something had to be done. Foot-braking power was the only solution. Either that or guide the bike into the hillside on the right or swing over an embankment and into a rice paddy on the left; I could hear the bones crunching and cracking. So those two courses of action were out. For a split second, the stream straight ahead looked inviting. But for only a flash, and I jammed my heels onto the roadway again. It was like putting them in a broiler from the intense heat from friction generated by the leather digging into the gravelly dirt.

The bike had begun to wobble by this time, and then all of a sudden the foot of the hill was right there, just a few feet away. Try to make the hairpin curve, or swing to the right for the bridge, or end up with a dunking? If I missed the bridge's roadway, crashing into the concrete posts would surely mean broken bones. A head-to-foot dunking in the deep, fast-moving stream was a frightening thought. I had never cared much for swimming. I shoved and tugged the handlebars to the left, aiming for the inside of the curve. With that, the front wheels began skidding in the pebbles and I went somersaulting over the handlebars. Somehow, some way in landing, my heels hit first and helped to break the fall.

Sister Teresa braked to a stop, let her bike fall to the road, and ran over to me. "Are you all right?" She was white as a ghost.

"Yes, I think so." Everything seemed hazy, and my body began to feel all achey and dish-rag limp. Even my stomach was doing somersaults by this time, and I started to quiver all over from nervous reaction.

"Can you move?"

"I think so. Let me try."

"Oh, no, don't!" She was frightened by her first suggestion as she now remembered a first-aid axiom: keep an accident victim quiet until bones can be examined for breakage. "Let me make sure you are all right."

"I'm not broken in any way, I think," and, stupidly ignoring the first-aid warning, I began moving my arms and legs and body. Fortunately, although strangely, there were no broken bones. There were some black and blue marks on the way; the heel of my left hand was cut apparently from hitting the road in a reflexive, bracing maneuver; and the right arm was skinned from the wrist to the elbow. Also quite fortunately, nothing on the bike or in the medical kit was broken either. I got up finally and brushed off my clothes. Sister Teresa cleaned out the cuts and bruises with some alcohol, and we went on to the sick mother. She survived, too.

"We've got to do something about this transportation problem," I said to Sister Teresa on our way back to the convent that night. "But what? That is the big question." Neither of us had a ready answer.

The idea did start to take shape, however, as the direct aftermath of a flash flood. I was in Sister Raphael's office doing some typing and did not pay any attention to a flash of rain coming down in sheets. Sudden, violent storms were not unusual. Then I felt my feet getting wet. Not just damp from the usual moisture in the cement floor. Within a matter of minutes, the water was swirling around my ankles. I reacted fast and broke for the screen door and the yard. The water was roiling all over the place and rising rapidly. Baskets, light bulbs and bamboo chairs floated around in the yard. And bugs, roaches the size of a canary and a few snakes struggling to keep from drowning.

Tons of water roared down the incline from the rear of the garden into our living quarters and on toward the front of the compound. There were a few small drainage holes in the wall, but this flash flood was too much for them and the backed-up water was rising at an unbelievably fast rate. Unless it had a way of escaping, its weight and pressure would tumble down the wall. But before that, the water would rise four or more feet inside the compound and destroy our clothing, furniture, bedding, bags of rice and other staples, and drown our chickens and possibly the pigs. I waded to the tool shed close-by, yanked out a sledge hammer, and waded, now knee deep, back to the wall and started banging away at the bricks. All around were bugs frantically trying to climb up the wall and an occasional snake wriggling by. I was so intent on breaking through the wall that I did not even give them a second thought. The bricks began giving way to the sledge's blows, a hole flew open, and the water gushed through. The water's pressure tore out more bricks to widen the gap. At that moment, the rain stopped as quickly as it had started. My arms and shoulders by this time were aching as though they were on fire from swinging the sledge. I relaxed, took a deep breath, looked around and saw the bugs and two snakes. It took only a split second to drop that sledge and head for the safety of the nearest building.

The sisters, meanwhile, were busy saving our wordly goods. Some were detailed to pull wearing apparel from the portable clothes closets and stack it high and dry on the closets' tops. Others went about saving books and church goods. Still others hurried into the kitchen and lifted hundred-pound bags of rice onto the brick stove. Some waded to the chicken coop to rescue chickens trapped in the water, and lifted them to safety on the perches. Another checked on the pig pen to make sure the pigs were all right.

The flood subsided as quickly as it had come up. Still, it took a few days to clean up the muddy mess. During the clean-up, I ran across some old magazines. In one of them was a picture of a Volkswagen station wagon. Like a flash, this was the answer to our transportation problems. Such a vehicle would serve a three-fold purpose: a mobile clinic, an ambulance and transportation for the sisters on trips to mission stations and other duties. We had talked off-handedly about buying a car if any money was left over after building the convent. The station wagon would be perfect—if we had had the money.

Regretfully, we were broke again. Even with some additional contributions that had raised our mother house fund over $30,000 it was going to be touch and go building our new home and furnishing it. When the original plans were drawn up in 1960, all of us overlooked one thing. There is always a price rise at the Chinese New Year. This is as traditional as firecrackers, dragons and burning of paper money during the celebration. In the meantime, there had already been one Chinese New Year, in 1961—and a price increase—and another observance in a few weeks. Our contractor gave us the sad news with the new estimates shortly before ground was broken on a two-acre site at the outskirts of Chiayi City in January, 1962. Instead of $30,000, the cost would be closer to $35,000. There would not be one red cent left over.

So, we went right on using our feet, bikes and public buses as our means of transportation in the medical work. But surely there had to be some way of getting our four-wheel transport. I started getting one of those money ideas again, and wrote a twin-purpose letter to Sister Catherine Chang, who was still in the United States. I asked her to drop around to the Catholic Medical Mission Board during a projected trip to New York and check out a list of medical supplies that we could use. I also suggested that in her travels she might run across somebody or an organization that would donate an ambulance or funds for one. I did not want to suggest a station wagon as that sounded too ritzy. An ambulance would be fine, too. It would be just dandy for our medical chores, and whenever the sisters had to go someplace they could ride in the back. Nonetheless, I preferred a Volkswagen station wagon for two reasons: one, its high wheel base was perfect for the deep-rutted country roads, and, secondly, it was good on gas mileage. I had no idea of what it would cost, and hurried a letter off to my brother Bill, who was then state editor of the *Bee* in Sacramento, California. He gave a figure of "around $1,500," and I sent the cost to Sister Catherine immediately so that she would have something to work with.

Sister Catherine is a fund-raising whiz. She had clicked with Cardinal Cushing the year before. Also, around that same time she had asked a priest-patient at St. Alexius Hospital in Bismarck to hold a special mission collection for

us. He did and raised nearly $800. Now she was going
to make another fund-raising try, this time for four-wheel
transportation. Sister Catherine was successful, as usual. It
so happened that somebody had given a charitable organization $1,500 earmarked for a foreign mission ambulance.
We were registered as a foreign missionary community,
and Sister Catherine's presentation of our needs resulted
in our getting the gift. My brother deserved to know about
our good fortune and have an opportunity, too, of sharing
in it.

"Dear Bill," I wrote from Mei-shan amid packing and
getting ready to move to our new mother house in September, "Will you scout around and see about picking up
a second-hand Volkswagen station wagon for the price
you mentioned before. Please make sure it is in good
condition. As soon as we receive a check for $1,500 from
a donor who wants to remain anonymous I'll let you know
so that you can close the deal. How should our check be
made out—to you or the dealer?"

Everything moved swiftly. We received the money. The
Taipei office of Catholic Relief Services-N.C.W.C. offered
to deliver the vehicle when it arrived in Taiwan, and also
would arrange with the government to admit it tax-free. I
had never thought of that! Back in California, Bill found
a wagon for about the amount we had received. He made
a good deal through a friend who worked for a used-car
dealer, and went ahead and signed all the papers in the
sales' transaction. The day Bill's letter with the good news
arrived, I went into Chiayi about one o'clock in the afternoon to arrange for the bank to send him the money. One
hour before, at twelve o'clock noon, the U. S. Military had
clamped down on transferring funds to the States, except for servicemen. I was totally unware of this until the
U. S. Military broke the bad news. I implored the banker
to grant a waiver on the grounds that we were a non-

profit organization that had been put in a very embarrassing position by the unexpected freeze. The banker made some telephone calls in our behalf, but no luck. The $1,500 could not be transferred.

What would Bill say when he heard about this! My brother had never been a foreign missionaryphile. In his letters about the station wagon, he never came right out and said it, but I got the impression that the only reason he became involved was to help his kid sister. His answer to my letter about the monetary embargo and the suggestion that he get a release from the car owner was not at all enthusiastic.

"The car's owner would not release me from the purchase," he wrote. "So I am stuck with the wagon. He also wants to be paid right now, and I am arranging for a $1,500 mortgage on the house to pay the bill."

Poor Bill. I felt awful. He had already gone out of his way to arrange for free transportation to Taiwan via the Navy's Operation Handclasp. This task had included writing letters to the two California United States Senators and his Congressman in efforts to clear away a lot of red tape. Bill technically was not our authorized agent in the United States and, therefore, not really eligible to use the free, transoceanic shipping services provided to nonprofit groups working in the foreign mission field. And now the money freeze had to happen!

The whole thing had turned into a mess, but there had to be a way out. I talked it over with Mother Philomena and received her permission to talk to a missionary priest with the Society of the Divine Word, which had its headquarters in the States. The idea was this: the Our Lady of China community would transfer the $1,500 to the S.V.D. order's use in Taiwan, and the S.V.D. in the United States would, in turn, send Bill a check for that amount. It was a simple matter of bookkeeping and was quickly approved.

We all felt much better until the weeks dragged into two months and Bill still had not received the check. It had been mailed to him. That much we knew from correspondence both with the order in Taiwan and the United States. Finally, after three months had elapsed, a dirty, beaten-up envelope was delivered to his house. It had been addressed correctly, the postmark was three months prior to date of delivery, but where it had gone astray and why it was in such a terrible condition nobody seemed to know. But more important, Bill had finally received the check.

It would be months before the wagon's arrival. Until then, we would go on using our feet, bikes, buses—and a motorcycle. The cycle was a gift from Father Sun. It was given to him originally in Hong Kong some years back when he was a newly-arrived refugee from Communist China. Sometimes at Mei-shan, when we would be setting out on one of our medical trips, my eyes looked longingly at the chain-drive machine parked outside the priest's room. I wondered what it would be like to strap the heavy medical case on the carrier, kick over the starter and go putt-putting away. No more walking, no more arduous biking or walking up hills and riding down, and no more playing sardine on crowded, stifling buses. I even dreamed in my sleep about Father Sun's motorized wheels after a back-breaking, leg-aching day.

Shortly after we moved into Chiayi in September of 1962, he bought a new motorcycle and turned his old one over to us. For an old bike rider like myself, switching to balancing on a motorcycle was no problem at all. It was a cinch to ride, but the very dickens to start. My leg would be about worn out from pumping the heavy starter before it would catch. On top of that, the cycle leaked oil. I never quite trusted it for long trips, except in extreme emergencies, because I was never positive about ever getting it started again, or that it would not run out of oil. So its use was limited pretty much to local calls in and around Chiayi City.

The first time I used the motorcycle for a long trip there was an awful tugging at my habit. In moments, the tugging became so pronounced that I began listing to the starboard. I got the cycle stopped, looked down, and there was the hem balling up in between the chain drive and sprocket. The hem was caught so badly that two hands were needed to work it loose. So much of the skirt was tangled up, however, that I could not maneuver to get at the kickstand, or even put the machine on its side without being bodily pulled to the ground with it. I was in an awful fix, sort of trapped in the saddle. The only way out of the dilemma was to have somebody hold the motorcycle while I eased myself out of the seat.

Quite a crowd had collected by this time in the typical Chinese fashion of gathering around to gape at somebody doing something or other a little bit out of the ordinary. Nobody, youngsters or grownups alike, said anything. They just stood there, heads bent forward a bit in their eagerness to see all. Nobody offered to help, either, for that would have meant my losing face.

Well, face or no face, this was a job that needed two hands to work the hem out of the sprocket and another pair to hold onto the cycle. I looked around the crowd. There was an elderly man standing in the group. He had the wispy, gray chin whiskers so often seen in Chinese classical art. He wore a long, black gown that came down to his ankles. He could have been a scholar or a merchant who had clung to the style of clothing worn for centuries by the Chinese men of rank, a style that had begun to give way rapidly to the Western business suit among the younger Chinese.

"Venerable one," I said, using the traditional, tactful style employed in addressing an elder. "Would you help me?"

"Honorable *ni-ku*," he said, "there are others here more worthy of assisting you than I."

He was not attempting to avoid helping, but was using the formal, polite speech of the Chinese people. Oh, no, I thought, all we need are two cups and a teapot and sit around for an hour or so in proper conversation before getting down to the facts at hand. On the other hand, it would have been insulting if I had used the direct, straight-to-the-point American approach, although in my discomfort, I was sorely tempted at the moment to do just that. But I followed the courtesies used by the people, but, at the same time, moved quickly to the point. He finally stepped forward, grasped the bike while I gingerly crawled off and bent over to extract the hem. It was so tangled that the job required quite a little time and still another extra pair of hands. I turned to a teen-age lad for the additional help. He looked alert, and also had not yet reached that stage in life where protocol was important to him. He pitched in, and we finally managed to get the job done, although the hem was torn and oil-soaked.

A few months after I had started motorcycling around Chiayi City, a friend said, "Sister, have you noticed something unusual on the streets lately?"

"No, nothing in particular; why?"

"Quite a few women have been seen driving motorcycles."

"What is so unusual about that?" I asked. We had not been living in the city that long for me to have taken much notice of individuality, or abrupt changes in the habits of the people. The city still seemed like a crowded maze, of throngs choking the streets, water-buffalo carts, scads of bicycles and oodles of scooters, scores of pedicabs, dozens of small, Japanese, barn-red taxis, vendors' signals, record players and radios tuned to the high-key, wailing Chinese opera. I had not been able to sort out the singularity of the streets—women's shops on one street of the business district, men's stores on another and so forth—the traffic, the noises, and the people in relationship to their stations in life by the quality and styling of their clothing. And especially whether more women than usual were driving motorcycles and scooters, as my friend had suggested.

"It is unusual because, until recently, only men drove the scooters and cycles," she said. "Women and teen-age girls rode sidesaddle as passengers. They must have thought that if you could do it, so could they. It is not a fad, either. It is part of the emancipation, the rapid Westernization that is going on among the younger Chinese, even instances of their having a say as to the pro and con of their parents' choice of a marriage mate."

I thought about all of that and then laughed in a joking way. "I never dreamed that I'd have an influence on an ancient and deep-rooted culture."

True or not, I was given a new name—*mo-t'o-ch'e tai fu,* the motorcycle doctor.

CHAPTER TEN

We moved into our new mother house in September of 1962. There was a feeling of awe, of disbelief among the sisters. Here, at last, was their permanent home, a two-story, light gray, crushed stone and brick building. The wonderment was greatest among those who had fled Shantung fifteen years before. Some hesitantly fingered the door frames, then let their hands run up and down the wood, feeling it, tapping it, turning to each other with expressions of pure joy.

"It is ours."

"I cannot believe this is true."

"Our prayers, our novenas have been answered."

They gingerly stepped on the terrazzo flooring, slowly caressed its hard smoothness with the soles of their black shoes, and finally tapped on it to make certain they were standing on something real, something solid that was theirs, and not some billowy, fleeting dream. The newer ones in the community—those of us who had joined at Mei-shan—were in awe, yes, after the miserable conditions in the mountains. Still, I doubt that any of us late-comers had quite the same deep, is-it-really-true sensation that had overpowered the older sisters from mainland China itself.

There was a mountain of work to be done in settling down in our new home: straightening up our rooms; arranging and rearranging our best but skimpy stock of furniture in the visitors' reception room so that it would not look too bare (the rest of the house—off-limits to all but sisters—was almost empty); unpacking dishes and chopsticks; storing the sacks of rice and other staples; hanging pictures and crosses; and scores of other moving-in chores. Yet, we could not resist the temptation of a quick, first-hand inspection tour of our still unlandscaped grounds, and a look around outside the compound that was surrounded by a six-foot brick wall. We shoved open the steel front gate onto *Fang Ts'ao Li,* Fragrant Grass Road. This was our postal address, and what a beautiful, exotic name it was! Well, maybe someday it would be all those lovely things. Right now it was not grassy green; it was a grassless, dirt foot-and-bicycle path along the edge of a shallow, eight-foot-wide stream in which the families living around us washed their clothing. The fragrant part? It came on an east wind from a fertilizer factory one short block away. On the other side of the stream was a huge, square field that ran a half mile in each direction. In a short while a combination, co-educational junior and senior high school would be built on the left end of the field, and a boys' senior high on the right. And each morning, when the classes assembled, the schools' bands would play catchy marching melodies as the young students went through exercises, capped by the stirring national anthem.

We walked back inside the compound and roamed around the grounds, looking first at the nearly an acre of land set aside for our vegetable garden and peanut "plantation" and then at another quarter acre for sweet potatoes. The latter would be fed to the pigs we intended to raise as soon as we could get together enough money to build the pens and also a modern, airy chicken house that would hold 250 egg-laying hens and replace a small, temporary coop off in a corner of the property. The garden, pigs and chickens would provide us with food and also an income from the sale of products. There was a raucous horn-tooting at the back gate. When the sisters swung open the double steel doors, a truck pulled in. It carried our fifty chickens from Mei-shan. The arrival of the cackling birds was a signaling reminder that it was time to get back to the work of moving in. We would be here a long, long time.

It did not seem possible that in less than nine months ground had been broken and a beautiful building had risen from the earth. Nor did it seem possible that near-tragedy and heartbreak had taken place in the construction. Father Sun nearly lost his life on one of his frequent trips to Chiayi to check on the progress of the work and quality of materials. A bus on which he was returning to Mei-shan was struck by a train at a blind mountain curve. A half dozen passengers were killed. Father Sun fortunately escaped with only severe cuts and bruises. His frequent trips were prompted principally by the job foreman whom we suspected of stealing us blind. The man's larceny was proven and a new foreman hired. He was a wiry little man and as honest as the day was long. Although he was not well, he was on the job from early morning to late at night. He had cancer and died shortly after the work was finished. He left a wife and four children, whom Mother Philomena took under her wing by sending them clothing and food, and some money whenever possible.

It did not seem possible either that within three months after we had moved in that disease would practically wipe out our flock of chickens again, and that thieves would scale the wall and steal the two still alive while all of us were at Christmas Eve midnight mass. Mother Philomena had planned to serve those two chickens as part of a real feast celebrating our first Christmas Day in Chiayi City.

That night, when we returned from the mass and learned of the theft, Mother Philomena's spirits dipped. She had labored hard to save the flock, and now there was not one left. This was not our only heartache since moving to Chiayi.

Brand new beds ordered especially for our new quarters had started falling apart. The carpenter had used fresh-cut wood. As it quickly dried out, the joints came apart, and almost every night for a week some sister went crashing to the floor. We were frightened to get into the beds until the carpenter reinforced them. Until then we went back to sleeping on our *tatamis* as we had done while waiting for the beds' delivery. Something had gone wrong with the specifications for the wood-burning water heater and there was never enough hot water to go around for showers and baths. There was even some whispered criticism of our community for having erected a "palace." It was as though we had usurped an honestly earned human right to some degree of comfort. And now thieves had come over the wall and literally stolen the *pièce de résistance* of our Christmas dinner. It seemed that the bleak days at Mei-shan had followed us.

While we were making plans for the new mother house two years before, we talked of perhaps building a hospital, too. Not a large one—maybe ten beds in conjunction with an out-patient clinic. This was not just some whim of a head-in-the-sky American female fresh from the States. It was based on simple logic. There were not enough good hospitals. All of them also had set fees, and it was only on rare occasions that we were able to have a critically ill patient admitted as a charity case. There were times patients could not be hospitalized because we did not have the money for their care or there were simply no beds available.

I can recall patients who died because of lack of hospital treatment. A thirty-two-year-old mother of four children was one of them. She came to us with an incipient case of pulmonary tuberculosis. Rest in a hospital and treatment with the wonder drugs would have arrested her ailment. Instead, she had to remain at home, where she worked hard, and steadily grew worse and finally died. A family brought prematurely born triplets to us at Mei-shan. They were bloated because of a lack of proper milk and round-the-clock hospital care. The mother and father were poor and we were not much better off than they financially. It was a shattering thing to stand by and be unable to do anything while they slowly died. There were also a number of patients whose recovery would have been speeded by a few weeks in a hospital. Instead, they had to suffer through a recovery period of months, and lost valuable time away from their work.

I was not alone in this desire for a small hospital. Many of the sisters from the mainland had worked in our hospital there and were hospital-trained in nursing. Their hearts bled at our inability to give more than clinic treatment. As much good as we did through our clinics, all of us felt we could do much more with our own hospital. The success of the mother house fund-raising program prompted me to broach the hospital subject in more concrete terms with Mother Philomena and Sister Raphael. In fact, there were two thoughts—one, the combination mobile clinic and ambulance, and, secondly, a ten-bed hospital and dispensary in Chiayi. I had already roughed up some plans and obtained estimates of around $5,000 to stock the hospital. Although, as things turned out, the mother house did cost more than we had planned on, I was still confident that we could scrape up the money somehow and began hunting for another American-trained nurse. A contact was made through the Catholic Medical Mission Board. Her name was Maryann Heim of Dubuque, Iowa, and a recent graduate of St. Anthony's School of Nursing in Rock Island, Illinois. Maryann wanted to go into lay missionary work for a couple of years. We started a correspondence and, in the end, she joined us in the forepart of November 1962. She was a godsend.

Maryann arrived when I was restricted to the mother house for two months prior to taking the first vows. Mother Philomena gave me special permission to go up to Keelung to meet the boat. Sister Raphael accompanied me. We were a little late in arriving, but when I saw this tall, red-haired American girl looking somewhat frantically around, I knew she was Maryann.

"Guess you thought we'd never get here," I called out breathlessly as Sister Raphael and I hurried through the milling knots of passengers and their welcoming committees of friends and relatives in the waiting room.

"Where have you been?" she blurted, as her blue eyes flashed with annoyance, and she stood inside a ring of luggage. Maryann was not one to mince words.

"We are terribly sorry," I said and introduced Sister Raphael. "We were caught in an awful traffic jam." Sister Raphael and I had stayed overnight at our mission in Chungli, and took a bus early in the morning for Taipei and changed to another bus for Keelung. Altogether, the distance was around fifty miles and traffic was murderous. I could understand Maryann's concern as only three years before I, too, had stood on this same dock, in the middle of hordes of Chinese all speaking a language that was foreign to me.

Maryann fitted in like a glove with everybody. She started taking Chinese lessons immediately. Sister Raphael became her teacher since I was still preparing for my vows. Also, because I was not permitted outside the compound until after the vows on December 8, there was nothing in the way of medical work for Maryann to do. In fact, the community's clinics were closed down for two months. So, when she was not studying, some of the sisters took her on tours of the countryside and Chiayi City itself. During one of her trips downtown, she ran into the *ch'ang-pi-tzu*, long nose, business. A little old lady, obviously senile, stopped and stared at her nose. Maryann still had not been introduced to the staring custom of the Chinese. She was embarrassed at first, then annoyed. She reacted as most Americans do.

"What are you looking at?" she finally asked.

Of course, the woman did not understand a word, but said something in return. Maryann's companion translated. "Is your nose real?"

Maryann frowned. "Certainly it's real. Why?" She still had not caught on to the fact that the Chinese, with their short and stubby noses, cannot imagine the Westerners' can be so big.

"May I touch it to make sure?" the woman asked.

By this time, Maryann's half-anger had turned to amusement. She thought it was some game the Chinese play and went along with the woman's question. "If you want to touch it, go ahead."

The woman slowly put her finger on the nose. She pressed in, and then from side to side. Her lips pursed in surprise. "It is real!" With that she hurried down the street, shaking her head in astonishment.

Back at the mother house, Maryann went into hysterics of laughter over the incident. "Did it ever happen to you?" she asked me.

"Sure. A few times. Down here in this part of Taiwan, there aren't many Westerners. They're sort of a novelty."

And then the Big Day—the first vows of poverty, chastity and obedience—arrived. I was scared stiff. Not from the fact that I would be making another giant step in devoting my life as a nun with the Sisters of Our Lady of China. Instead, fright over whether I would be able to read and pronounce all the Chinese characters correctly during the ceremony. It was in Chinese, except for the Latin portions of the mass. There is one thing about the Chinese language that drives Westerners crazy. It is the inflection. One word can mean many different things simply by a slight switch in the word tone. For instance, *t'ang* (*yen*) can mean soup or sugar, cigaret or salt, by changing the inflection. Fortunately, everything worked out fine. I was now formally Sister Mary Paul. I cannot recall a happier and more soul-satisfying day. I was floating on Cloud Nine, and have never come down. In another nine years, in 1971, I would take my final vows. During the interim, there would be a renewal of the vows. In our community, we do that every year for three years and then twice triennially.

The time had come to go back to work. Even though lack of money sent the ten-bed hospital down the drain, we decided to open a three-day-a-week clinic in Chiayi. The diocese owned a small, one-story, frame building in a solid row of open-front stores in the downtown section. It had been used for a while by another group of sisters as an eye clinic and then was closed down because the sister in charge had been transferred to another city.

Unlike the orderly, departmentalized nature of much of the downtown shopping area—men's clothing on one street, women's on another, and so forth—the clinic's street was a conglomeration of small businesses that included a metal-working shop next door, a photo-supply dealer, a jeweler, a beauty shop, barber shop, a couple of night clubs, a radio and record store, and some restaurants that also had competition from street vendors who sold steaming noodles, rice and sweet potatoes from their pushcarts. The street itself, crowded from morning to night with pedestrians, bicycles, scooters, pedicabs and an occasional horn-honking taxi, was about twenty feet wide and bordered on each side by deep gutters. These were actually sewers—typical of those used by the Chinese for centuries—closed over by planking fitted together to form a cover and keep people from falling in.

The clinic building itself was about a dozen feet wide

and fifteen feet deep. Not big, true, as even a waiting room in most State-side clinics, but it was a milestone in our eyes. It was in the heart of the city, right in the thick of things. That is how and where the Our Lady of China community wanted to be, in a place where we had a real chance to carry on an apostolate and expand our work for Christ.

A carpenter built cabinets for our medicines and instruments. We put up partitions for a narrow waiting room across the front, and back of that an examination room on one side, a pharmacy on the other, plus a laboratory stretching across the rear of the building. Walking space was at a premium, and two—not three—became a crowd in each partitioned-off area. We spent days scrubbing the floors, walls and ceilings and applying coats of cream-colored paint. Not white. Never, for that, in the Buddhist faith, is the sign of death, of mourning for the dead. We borrowed a truck and brought in supplies stored at Mei-shan and the new mother house.

The clinic was opened for business right after Christmas. Dr. Wang Hung Tu consented to become its director and consultant. At first, the caseload was light since we were still not well known in the city. The reason was simple enough: we had never worked there in a medical sense, although there were patients who traveled from Chiayi up to Mei-shan. The fantastic Chinese grapevine went to work, however, and within two weeks we were busy, with people lining up long before we opened at nine o'clock in the morning. In fact, we were swamped and took care of one hundred and more patients a day.

The original plan called for Maryann to handle the downtown clinic alone as soon as she picked up enough Chinese, while Sister Teresa Chan and I would resume our trips to the other dispensaries in the diocese. That plan had to be drastically revised. The caseload in Chiayi became too heavy for one person. At the same time, the sisters themselves were spread so thin in a myriad of other duties that not a single one could be spared to work with Maryann. There were times, too, when Sister Teresa was not available and Maryann would go along on the bus trips to our other clinics. We finally worked out a tight schedule that had us in Hsinkong on Monday, Chiayi on Tuesday, Mei-shan and Talin on Wednesday, Chiayi on Thursday, Touliu on Friday and Chiayi on Saturday.

One of our first Chiayi patients—and no doubt one of the biggest boosters on the grapevine—was a pork merchant. He suffered from narcolepsy and would sleep as much as twenty hours a day. The ailment was so far progressed that he would fall asleep standing behind the counter while customers clamored to be waited on. When he first started coming into the clinic he would drop off as soon as he sat down in the waiting room. The first time he came in, I heard this loud snoring. It sounded like wood being sawed. More out of curiosity than anything else, I stopped an examination of a patient and walked forward to the waiting room. Here was this huge man—in girth, that is—snoring away. He weighed close to 250 pounds.

"Maryann," I called out. "Come here a minute. I need some help." I had tried to awaken him but with no luck. I had hollered close to his ear and shook him. The metal workers next door had set up an ear-splitting din that burst right through the wall. The man just kept right on snoring away. Maryann and I finally got him awake by tugs at his shoulders and slapping his face.

He told us that he had been to doctors from Taipei down to the southern seaport city of Kaosiung, but nobody could do anything for him. As he talked about his problems, boom! he would be off to sleep. We began his treatment with amphetamine and B-complex vitamins. There was improvement almost immediately. He was overjoyed and began telling everybody about the "miracle doctor." This merchant came to us over a four-month span, by the end of which time he was wide awake, working all day, and sleeping around eight hours each night. He was living a normal life. Incidentally, he continues to come in for treatment whenever he begins to feel abnormally sleepy.

In one very important way, we were fortunate that he did come to us and that we were successful, since we began having problems with some of the local doctors. Most of the physicians were not concerned about us; some even welcomed our clinic because there were more than enough patients for them to handle. All of those physicians were concerned with sickness in a humane sense; they considered people's health of paramount importance. There was, however, a highly vocal few who wanted us out of business. This group saw only a "threat" to their livelihood. They tried to have us shut down by a whispering campaign that (1) we were quacks; (2) we used inferior medicines; (3) a lot of our patients died; and (4) we were subversively trying to sway the people against Buddhism. All of that was, of course, sheer nonsense. Our pork merchant patient seemed to take this smear campaign as a personal affront. He bought a two-column advertisement in the leading newspaper to tell his story about how we had brought him back from the somnolent world. His generous, unsolicited effort did much to give us stature in Chiayi.

In spite of the heavy work schedule that took all of our time, energy and thoughts, we had not entirely forgotten about the Volkswagen station wagon. We just did not know where it was, except in a general sense, namely, somewhere between Sacramento and Taiwan. Nobody could pinpoint its exact location or time of arrival. Inquiries brought back replies that it was on its way. Nothing more. Meanwhile, each bus trip with the heavy medical cases made us pray that much harder for it to come soon, and the sooner the better.

There was one particularly trying day at the Hsinkong clinic in mid-January of 1963. It was chilly when we left early in the morning and we wore extra wraps. The buses were unusally crowded, if that were possible. The day suddenly turned hot and muggy, and we were even more uncomfortable in the heavy clothing. Our medical cases seemed to weigh a ton and just about pulled the arms out of their sockets. The patients were knee deep and cranky about who was first. We arrived back at the mother house about eight o'clock that night, dead tired. The cook (we had taken on a new one right before we had moved from Mei-shan and her title was a horrible misnomer) had forgotten to leave us anything to eat. We were too worn out to bother cooking, and nibbled on some soggy rice the cook had stuffed away in the refrigerator, a large model that had been donated by Mr. Anderson's mother.

"I'm taking a shower and falling into bed," Maryann mumbled and slowly unwound herself out of the chair.

"Uh, huh," I grunted. "I'll do that later, after prayers and some letters that have to get out in the morning."

It was truly an effort to climb up to the second floor to my room. I had hardly settled down at the writing table when there was a light tapping on the door. It was Mother Philomena. Her face was aglow with excitement.

"Sister—sister." She kept her excited voice low because we were practicing silence and everybody else had long since retired. "There is a man downstairs. He brought the station wagon."

"No!" I yelled, completely forgetting that silence was in order. I quickly caught myself and murmured, "I'll be right down," and hurried downstairs to tell Maryann the good news. She did not even bother to rinse off the soap or towel herself dry before scrambling into a housecoat.

The man was a representative of Catholic Relief Services-N.C.W.C. in Taipei. He had picked up the wagon that morning on the dock at Keelung, cleared it, duty-free, through customs and drove it down for personal delivery.

Within a matter of minutes, we had raced to the rear of the mother house and stood gaping in wonderment and joy. There, under the harsh glow from a naked 100-watt night light, stood our station wagon nine feet tall. We were no longer tired. We were so keyed up that we could have worked the night through and still felt fresh as daisies.

"Look at that sweet, sweet baby," Maryann gasped. From that moment on, our wagon had a name, "Baby." That is all we ever called it. Except at times when it got balky and Maryann temporarily rechristened it with some less affectionate names.

I crawled up into the driver's seat, started the engine, and listened to that sweet, purring sound. What a joy to hear that! No more crowded buses, no more lugging medical cases, no more walking, no more bicycle or motorcycle jouncing. We had our own motor-drive four wheels at last.

When Pop had taught me to drive about ten years before in Illinois, he lectured constantly against "brake and horn drivers."

"If you drive carefully, observe all the traffic signs and the traffic laws, and have your car under control at all times, you can forget about the horn and avoid a lot of quick and unnecessary braking," he would say. "If I had my way, they'd take the horns off every automobile and truck. Too many drivers think that a horn gives them the right of way. That's another reason for a lot of accidents."

I wondered if Pop would change his tune if he were to come to Taiwan. A horn was equally as important, it seemed, as a gas pedal and brakes and steering wheel. People on the streets or walking on the highways simply would not see a car—or would ignore it, perhaps—and did not move aside unless they were honked down. Yet, as a passenger theretofore, I often wondered if all the horn-honking were really necessary. It always seemed that drivers got great delight out of using the horn instead of a slower speed or their brakes. That surmising was, of course, from purely a passenger's point of view. As a first-time, behind-the-wheel driver in Taiwan the next morning for the trip to the downtown clinic, I quickly changed my thinking. The horn was the only way to open up a passageway through the heavy foot and cycling traffic.

All of us at the convent quickly fell to in reconstructing the wagon's interior for use as an ambulance. We were, after all, no strangers to hammers, wrenches and screwdrivers; we had to learn to use the tools at Mei-shan or suffer through more disrepair to the buildings, water lines and so forth. We rearranged the wagon's seats to provide space for a stretcher, our medical cases, and a resuscitator our American servicemen friends at Taipei had bought for the ambulance. We contacted an auto body shop about repainting the wagon gray with a big white cross on each side. In the excitement of having our wagon, I had temporarily forgotten the significance the Buddhists put on white; perhaps ninety per cent of our patients followed that faith. The oversight did not matter much anyhow, since we had to change the color almost immediately because government regulations called for a green cross on all ambulances.

Baby's baptism of fire was not, oddly enough, in medical work. Its first major use was as a temporary refuge from one of the most severe earthquakes in twenty-seven years on the island. It rattled us shortly after the wagon's delivery.

We had returned late from the clinic that evening of the quake, and I was not feeling well. Mother Philomena said that as soon as my prayers were finished that I should go right upstairs to bed. She attempted to rush me through the prayers, but I was a trifle slow, as I had a strong desire to linger in the chapel. I had just begun to stand up when the quake struck, knocking me to the floor. Pews toppled and other sisters were knocked down just like rows of ten pins. The lights went out instantly, and we were in total darkness. The floors continued to tremble violently and there was a continuous roar from windows and statues and whatever else was movable crashing to the floor. I could hear a sister in the front moaning and I thought a wall had caved in on her. A toppling pew had struck her in the small of the back, inflicting, fortunately, only a painful bruise. I tried to get up but the trembling underfoot was so great that it knocked me right down. Others all around me were having the same problem. I remember at that moment feeling as if the end were there and was amazed how calmly I was taking it all. It was the first time in my life that I felt close to death.

The pitching and rolling continued for several minutes. Nobody could get off the floor. There were moans from several novices and prayers from the sisters. And then the terrible shaking and rumbling finally stopped. Everyone scrambled to his feet and stumbled through the pitch darkness to the doors. As we ran through a corridor to the outside, the floor under us began to shake again and it was like running on something that was not there. We expected the building to start falling down on us, and we hurried to the most open part of the grounds to get clear of any flying debris.

There was no moon that night, but off in the distance there was a long wall of flames that seemed to stretch about five or six blocks across the business district. The flames burst high in the sky and appeared to be spreading quickly. As we gathered together and babbled excitedly in our shock, a high-pitched hissing sound could be heard of gas escaping from the bottled gas tank on one side of the mother house. We were frightened at this new danger, the possibility of its exploding and blowing the house and us sky high. Some of us groped through the darkness to the tank. It had been knocked over and the rubber tubing broken off. It took a few minutes to find the valve handle and shut off the flow. By the time we were finished, I, at least, was soaking with perspiration from fear. Later, we learned there really was no danger attached to the task.

For some unknown reason, all of us migrated to the station wagon, which was parked in a large, open spot back of the convent. There were seventeen of us—nuns, novices and aspirants—at the convent. Except for some bruises, none of us was seriously hurt. We hovered around that wagon as though it were the mother hen and we were the chicks. Outside the compound, there were screams as the frightened people ran from their one-story frame homes. We could hear the horrible sounds of ripping wood and thunder-clapping crash as houses, already weakened, toppled into piles of rubble during fresh tremors. The wide glare of flames broadened in the downtown sky, and other fires sprang up throughout the city, some of them close to the mother house. Some of us wanted to go out and help, but Mother Philomena refused permission.

"There is nothing we can do right now, and we would endanger our own lives from the many fallen electrical wires," she explained.

That night, all seventeen of us crowded into the station wagon to sleep. How did we all get in? I do not know, and nobody else could explain it. Yet, we managed. Nobody wanted to sleep inside the mother house. Our staying in the wagon was a case, I imagine, of a feeling of security, of safety in numbers, as the tremors went on through the night.

With the break of dawn, we dragged our cramped bodies from the wagon, and one of our first thoughts was how the mother house fared. It stood up quite well considering the severity of the first quake and the many medium-intensity tremors that followed during the night. The upper rim around the building had cracked off, and there was some damage to the exterior and interior walls. There was a large crack in the roof.

Even while we surveyed the damage, the small tremors continued to take place. Incidentally, they went on at infrequent and less-recurring intervals for nearly a month. If we were in the convent when a quake started, we would scamper outdoors. A couple of times I said, "Hey, stop, you don't have to worry about this one." But as I was saying it, I was running, too. It was just a matter of the legs reacting before the mind got the true picture that the rumbling was not serious. The station wagon, meanwhile, continued as the dormitory for some of us for a week. Each night more would decide to return to their own beds, but a few of us were reluctant about going back to our rooms until we were positive the tremors had stopped for good. I could not bring myself to return to my second-floor room for about a month and took quarters temporarily on the first floor. In my case, it was just pure fright of what might happen with the already damaged roof if another severe quake hit. I just did not fancy its falling in on me.

While at breakfast the morning after the big quake, my chopsticks stopped in mid-air. "The clinic!" I exclaimed. Everybody around the table stopped and stared at me.

"What about the clinic?" one of the nuns asked.

"That big fire downtown last night—did it get to the clinic?" And then I thought of something else. "Or did the earthquake destroy it first?"

As soon as breakfast was over, some of us piled into the wagon and headed for the business district. We drove only a few dozen feet beyond our gate when we began seeing the quake's destructive effects. Utility poles were down or leaning crazily. Wires were snaked around in the streets.

Many houses had collapsed; many others were twisted out of shape. Police and soldiers turned back sightseers and re-routed people with legitimate business via a crazy-quilt pattern of roundabout streets. A ride that normally required only about ten minutes now took nearly an hour.

We had to park about a block away from the clinic and pick our way through the debris. We could see from that distance that our building and those around it were still up. As we got closer, we could see that a beam that supported one end of the front part of the clinic had buckled, but there was no immediate danger of collapsing. The building itself was otherwise intact. Some of the others on the block were down. A few were lopsided, but at least half the buildings had survived, like ours, with only minor damage. The huge fire that we had seen from the convent the night before had been choked off more than a block away after destroying an area of a half dozen city blocks. Police, fire-men and soldiers were everywhere, digging into the rubble, bringing in bulldozers and mechanized scoops and dump trucks to begin the job of cleaning up.

We hurried into the clinic, expecting to see the worst from all the glass bottles and jars stored in the cabinets and on the shelves. We were not at all disappointed. A heavy, sweep aroma of raspberry was in the air. It came from a broken bottle of liquid medicine. The amber, syrupy fluid had run every which way and begun to dry into a sticky mess. Glass from broken medicine bottles, and thousands of pills and vitamin capsules were all over the floor. Our clinic stocks had been nearly exhausted by the quake. We were heartsick, as medicine was hard to come by free and in large quantities from the States and almost prohibitive in price when bought on the local market. In fact, some of the de-stroyed medicines had just been bought locally to tide us over until a shipment arrived from Mr. Anderson. He had written that he had shipped a few barrels of samples he and our other friends in the United States had collected, but there was no indication when they would arrive. All we had left were some medicines stored, and intact, at the mother house. There was enough for another three weeks.

We walked gingerly through the glass, pills, capsules and liquid to the laboratory in the backroom. Strangely, it was all right except that a two-gallon bottle of distilled water sat upright in the middle of the concrete floor.

"Maryann, was that bottle sitting there when we left here last evening?" I was positive that everything was in proper order, as we made it a practice of having things shipshape for the start of our next clinic day.

"No," she said. "It was on the bench."

"That's strange." I thought of the possibility of looters having broken in as an aftermath of the earthquake. Maybe they had dragged it off the bench but were frightened away and left it on the floor. Still, a quick glance showed the equipment was still there—the microscope, test tubes, slides and so forth.

I walked over to the door that opened onto the narrow alleyway leading into a side street. The door was still bolted from the inside. Our front door also was locked when we had arrived. That ruled out looters. The only thing we could figure out was that the bottle had "walked" off the bench during the sharp tremors and plopped onto the floor.

"This is crazy," Maryann laughed. "Do you remember about a month ago how that other bottle was set down on the floor a little too hard and shattered into a zillion pieces?"

Strange, strange things happen during earthquakes.

Right now, there was only one thing to be done—a thorough housecleaning. We drove back to the convent and loaded up with brooms, shovels, buckets, rags and soap. We had a long, long day of hard work ahead of us. Within a half hour of our return, a young man came to the door and stared at us on our hands and knees and washing up sticky medicine. We figured he was doing what came naturally, staring, and did not bother to look up from our work. He must have stood there a good ten minutes before he spoke.

"Can you fix me?"

His trousers were in shreds; his legs were crisscrossed with scabs of coagulated blood. He had been cut while tugging his legs free from walls that had collapsed in his parents' home near the clinic. Other earthquake victims began straggling in. Cuts, bruises and burns made up most of the cases. Then a little girl walked in. A finger had been amputated. The stub was covered with a filthy rag. The child never once uttered so much as a whimper while we cleaned and dressed the amputated joint, an agonizingly painful experience for any amputation victim. Her stoicism was typical of all the Chinese in times of personal physical suffering. Several people came in with broken arms, wrists and fingers. We referred them to hospitals, which we could imagine were already overburdened with quake victims. Yet we could not safely handle these fracture cases because we had no X-ray equipment to determine the extent of the breaks and precise location for setting.

Within a few days, and our clinic spic and span again, we got back to the normal run of patients, the heart cases, high blood pressure, worms, ulcers, goiters, trachoma, malnutrition and on and on through the host of diseases and ailments. I began to worry. Our medication supplies were dwindling rapidly, and I was concerned that we would have to close down the clinic for a while. I sometimes used an expression, "the Holy Ghost was sitting on my shoulder," when a patient with a particularly difficult ailment responded nicely. I had occasion to use it again in another sense on two occasions. The first time was the arrival of the Chinese New Year. Absolutely nobody was sick for two weeks. That gave us a welcome extension in hope that Mr.

Anderson's shipment would show up in another few weeks at the most. The second time the Holy Ghost sat on my shoulder was right after the New Year. Mr. Anderson's barrels arrived, and fears of having to close down for lack of supplies vanished just as quickly as the earthquake had set them in motion.

So, it was business as usual, and there was never a dearth of that.

CHAPTER ELEVEN

The role of Cupid is not generally associated with a nun's life. We have our moments, too, however. Mine came because of a brickyard accident. Sister Teresa, Maryann and I were closing up the Chiayi clinic for a dinner break about one o'clock in the afternoon when the romance role had its start. A local doctor requested that we check out his diagnosis of a patient, a teen-age girl who had been brought in from the country. Her right leg was badly infected, so far gone that she needed hospitalization.

We explained to the mother that the only way to save her daughter's life was by getting her to a hospital quickly. We also cautioned that the leg might have to be amputated. Privately, we were practically certain that the infection was so far advanced and her condition so critical that her only chance of survival was through removal of the leg. The mother agreed to everything we told her. We eased her daughter onto the stretcher and into our ambulance.

On the way to the hospital an hour or so away she told us her name was Mei-ling and that she was eighteen years old. Her father had been killed in a fight. Her mother, who worked at the brick factory, became so depressed by his death that she was unable to work. Mei-ling took her place. She was assigned to a large, electrically driven machine that chopped up clay. Mei-ling was not too familiar with the machine, and, somehow, her leg became caught. A steel claw ripped it from the foot to the hip. A country doctor, not knowing what he was doing, decided to sew up the wound. In so doing, he also sewed off a vein. Circulation was cut down, and the leg became badly infected. The mother finally arranged to take her to the doctor in Chiayi, but, by this time, the poor girl was running a high fever and her leg was badly infected.

During the drive to the hospital, we joshed with Mei-ling to keep her spirits up. Sister Teresa teased her about having a boy friend, and Mei-ling, a pretty, doe-faced girl, turned crimson.

"Ah-hah," Sister Teresa said. "Now we know your secret. You are going to be married."

Mei-ling dropped her eyes and smiled shyly.

"When is the wedding?" Sister Teresa asked, seriously. "And may we come and see the beautiful bride and the handsome husband?"

"Oh, yes." Mei-ling was pleased. "Would you really come to my wedding?"

Our fears about amputation were correct, but Mei-ling did not want to go through with it. "I will never be married," she cried. "No man will have me. I will be a cripple. I will never have children."

We explained that the most inportant thing in her life at that moment was getting well.

"Your boy friend loves you, doesn't he?" I asked.

"Yes, but not without a leg."

"Are you sure?"

"I think so. Yes."

"But you are not positive."

"Yes . . . no. Oh, please, I do not know for sure." A few tears trickled down Mei-ling's cheeks.

"Unless you get well," I persisted, "you will never know, will you?"

That seemed to clinch the argument. Mei-ling agreed to go through with the operation. Afterward, she went into a withdrawal stage that is not uncommon among amputees in their early post-operative period. She did not want to see her fiancé. She was now, in her eyes, a hopeless cripple, not worthy of a husband. She was withdrawn around her family, fearful that she had become a useless, nonproductive burden. We could read her thoughts—in the end she would become a beggar, dragging herself through the village with a hand outstretched and pleading for a little rice.

"How do you know your friend will not marry you?" I asked during a visit.

"I cannot let him see me like this. Anyhow, I know he will not marry me. I am a cripple." She was bitter.

"Did he tell you he wouldn't?"

"No."

It was time to shake her loose from self-pity and I deliberately lit into her. "You are a coward!" She did not expect to hear that, and flinched and drew away on the bed. "You will not let your fiancé come here and tell you whether he will marry you. You will not permit the hospital to fit you with an artificial leg so that you can walk again without crutches. Only a coward acts that way."

"I am not a coward." She was defiant. "Did I not agree to the operation? That took courage."

I grunted. "Children and babies go through worse operations than yours. So that's not a sign of courage. Facing up to your responsibilities as a daughter in an honorable family, as the fiancée of an honorable young man from a respected family—that is what takes courage." I started toward the door.

"Wait." It was almost a whisper.

"Wait for what? We have done all we can for you. Whatever happens after this is strictly up to you. Good-by." It was a cruel thing to do, but Mei-ling had reached an emotional period where babying would have done immeasurable, perhaps irreparable, harm.

"Wait." Her voice was sharp, more like a command than a plea. "This leg you talk about. How do I get one?"

I was in the doorway now, and turned around to face her. "I have already told you how. You can get it if you want it."

Mei-ling got her leg. And got her man, too. The last time the word reached us on the grapevine, she had given birth twice. Her husband was pleased and proud. She had produced two sons.

Around the time Mei-ling was operated on—it was not long after we received the ambulance—we had another hurry-up case for Baby. It was on a Sunday, our day off, of course, when word came that a thirteen-year-old girl was critically ill high up in the mountains. It was more than an hour's drive to the village. When we arrived, it was obvious that we were expected. One of the village elders in the crowd that gathered around the ambulance told us quickly how to reach the girl's house. It was about a half mile up the mountainside. The path was just wide enough for Baby to get through. It had rained hard during the morning and the mountain road was slippery in addition to being rutty and rocky. The road suddenly narrowed into a rocky foot path. Shanks' mares went back to work. Sister Teresa, Maryann and I lugged the stretcher and medical kits up the steep path. It became more rocky and steep as we climbed. We were just about played out when we arrived at the house. It was a mud and bamboo structure. The girl was on a pallet and obviously very ill. She said her name was May-hwa.

She worked at collecting bamboo branches to help supplement the family's meager income. One of the bamboo shoots, which are sharp as razor blades, had pierced her foot. Ten days later, she came down with tetanus. We had to be especially careful in moving her, as the slightest jolt could send her into convulsions. We gave her a large dose of phenobarbital to offset the possibility of convulsions. Naturally, getting her down the mountain on a stretcher was a harrowing experience for us all. As I pointed out before, the path was narrow, steep and rocky and slippery from the rain. Sister Teresa, Maryann and I felt like wrung out dish-rags by the time we reached the ambulance. Fortunately, our patient did not react badly to the stretcher ride.

There was no way to turn the ambulance around on the narrow road. That meant I had to back it more than two hundred yards to the macadam highway running through the village. The distance seemed more like two hundred miles. Sister Teresa and Maryann stayed in the back of the ambulance to keep the patient as comfortable as possible and also be prepared in case she went into a convulsion. We still had sixty miles to go before arriving at the hospital in Kaosiung. We could not hurry because the ride had to be smooth. In fact, I held the speed well under forty miles an hour and slowed down to a crawl in going over bumps. Even so, the girl did go into convulsions on the way. But there was an emotionally and spiritually rewarding ending to the story. Although most tetanus cases die, our patient lived. One of the big reasons was that we had an ambulance to get her to a hospital quickly. Otherwise, she surely would have died.

We were proud of Baby. Sister Raphael, though, had her doubts. They developed one night when Sister and I were returning from Talin in connection with a nonmedical errand for the community and also a fresh paint job on the front fender. It had been badly scraped while pushing a stalled car in Chiayi, and we did not want Baby ever to appear in any way but her best bib and tucker. The countryside was pitch black. We were kiting along at over forty miles an hour, since the road was good, smooth macadam. It was tree-lined, which, by the way, is a scenic feature of many of Taiwan's highways. I had learned, however, to keep an eye on the trees because people had a habit of darting out of the fields, either on foot or bicycle, and across the roadway before you could say Jack Robinson. The trees shielded them from view, and stopping in time could be touch and go. Whether on foot or bike, the people had a firm conviction about right-of-way—their own, of course.

On this particular night, the ambulance's headlight picked up a farmer scooting out on his headlightless bike a hundred feet away. I jammed on the brakes and, at the same time, sent the ambulance toward the road's shoulder in case there was not sufficient stopping room. With that, he did a quick turnabout, right into the ambulance's path. By some miracle, we stopped just as the bumper nudged the bike. The farmer fell lightly to the ground, jumped up, grabbed his bike, muttered over and over that he was not hurt and quickly pedaled away.

I felt like a piece of jelly and slumped back in the driver's seat, breathed a sigh of relief, and thought how lucky we were to have such good brakes. I turned to Sister Raphael and tried to make a joke. "I sure braked fast that time."

Sister Raphael, who had never driven any sort of motorized machinery, was not at all happy. "You say you braked —braked, that is the right word, yes?" she asked and went right on, "These brakes you talk about, they must not be very good or you would have stopped sooner and not hit that man."

There was no use going into a debate about it. Baby, herself, did not fare too well, either. Her nice, new fender paint job was streaked again. Well, that was bound to be Baby's life—a little scratch here, a little dent there, a little bit of colic in the gas line, a flat tire or two on a trip. It was all in a day's work, and Maryann would rechristen Baby with fiery tones and chastise her with a couple of bangs of the hand. Baby would whimper, and chug along fairly quietly until the next temper tantrum.

The ambulance and Chiayi clinic gave the Our Lady of China community's medical work additional stature. When we got the ambulance, I could sense a subtle change in the people's attitude. We had a feeling that they accepted our ministrations with more respect, as though the ambulance were some sort of status symbol that made us more important in their eyes. This led, of course, to more word-of-mouth advertising among the patients, swelling our caseload.

Additionally, there was a permanency about the Chiayi clinic because it was open three days a week, as opposed to the tenuousness of some of our other clinics. I have to take some of the blame for the latter. We had opened one-day-a-week clinics at various times in about a dozen, scattered towns, but had to close most of them because of either horrible bus transportation prior to the ambulance's arrival, not enough drug supplies to keep some of them open, or too much work and never enough time. Even after we had settled finally on a hard core of towns like Hsinkong, Meishan and Touliu, there was some suspicion that we might pack up and go elsewhere. After all, there was the grapevine that carried the news, true or not. Chiayi, on the other hand, gave us a solid base of operations, and some patients showed it in by-passing clinics closer to their homes and coming by bus, bike, or motor scooter—and sometimes on foot—into Chiayi.

Little Mike's grandmother was one. She brought him in from near Touliu, about twenty miles from Chiayi. She came by bus, carrying Little Mike in her arms. When I asked why she had not gone to our Touliu clinic, she became tight-lipped, saying only, "I come here." The hidden meaning was that she did not entirely trust Touliu's permanency, but was confident that we would never close the Chiayi clinic.

Little Mike himself was floppy limp, like a carrot that had

been out in the sun for a couple of days. He could neither stand, sit, nor talk. He was one of the worst malnutrition cases I have ever seen. He was not quite two and a half years old, so close to death that all of us in the clinic were half afraid to give him even a spoonful of watered-down milk for fear that his fleshless, bony body would fall apart from retching that might result from the shock of nourishment reaching his stomach. In cases such as this, food actually can cause death.

Needless to say, Little Mike was from a poor family. He and his three older brothers lived with a widowed grandmother. The mother had tuberculosis and left the family; the father was out of work.

Little Mike—his Irish-pug nose made him look as though his name should be Mike—needed hospital care, months of it if he could survive the first days of taking food. No hospital would take him that long without payment, and we did not have the money. It would have been a simple matter to give the grandmother some food, as a token treatment, send her on her way with the child and let him die. He really had only a few days of life left as it was. Such a course of action would have been criminal. Where there is even a faint spark of life, there is always hope that it can be fanned into full bloom again.

There was only one thing to do—take Little Mike out to the convent and begin working on him. It was touch and go at first, but he finally started to respond. In two months, he was much better and beginning to learn to walk. He was also sassy as a playful pup, and a bit spoiled, too. After all, he had about twenty "mothers" fussing over him, and, like all youngsters, soon learned that if one said no to one of his whims, another would say yes. But we loved this tyke. He was so cute, so full of life that we wanted to keep him forever. That, of course, was impossible. The word had already spread about Little Mike's presence at the mother house, and efforts were being made to pawn off unwanted children on us. As much as we wanted to have one, we were not in any position to start an orphanage. So, we took a very healthy Little Mike back to his grandmother, dropped off a month's supply of food, and said we would return with more. We were confident that, given half a chance, he would grow up into a fine, productive and useful citizen.

Within three weeks, the grandmother was back at the clinic in Chiayi with Little Mike in her arms. His eyes were sunken; the cheeks were no longer round and firm, but hollow and flabby; his arms and legs were skin and bone; and his body was hot with fever.

"Mike," I gasped, "whatever have they done to you!"

His mouth hung open, flaccid; and he stared blankly.

"What happened? What's wrong?" I asked the grandmother.

"He is sick. You take him." With that, she laid him in my arms. He was like a featherweight. I started toward the examination room. We had to find out what his symptoms were before we could start treatment. It just did not dawn on us that his problem was malnutrition again.

When Little Mike and the month's supply of food arrived back at the grandmother's house, she sat down and considered the survival chances of the four grandchildren. The three older children had a chance. Little Mike, no. He had already been at death's door. Therefore, he could not be healthy enough to live much longer. Moreover, he was just one more mouth to feed. Why, therefore, waste food on Little Mike when it would be more beneficial to the older children? It was a time-honored philosophy of survival of the fittest. Little Mike drew the short end of the straw in the rugged game of life; he would not get the food. A Westerner might think the grandmother was being heartlessly cruel. In her eyes, though, she had acted wisely. Her wisdom had grown out of hunger; it was an old, old story in the East.

We took Little Mike back to the convent. In a few weeks, he was as sassy as ever. When we returned him to the grandmother, we changed tactics. She had to bring him to the Catholic Church in Touliu every day for feeding. No Little Mike, no food. He is now in kindergarten. He looks as though he'll turn into a fine broth of a man.

Little Mike was not our only medical case. Heavens no! He was only one five-hundredths of the weekly caseload. That's right; we often averaged about 500 patient visits a week at the five clinics, and a few dozen house calls. The house calls were a respite, in a way, as they gave us a chance to get away from the clamor and crowds at the clinics. The calls were not always conducive to our good health, though. Such as around the time we finally got things squared away with Little Mike. Maryann and I were at the Talin clinic and were just about set to take a lunch break— and we were famished—when somebody rushed in and said a farmer had had a bad accident, please hurry. We hopped in Baby and raced about five miles outside the city. The farmer had fallen off a motorcart stacked with sacks of rice, and a back wheel ran over him. There were no broken bones, but the man was in pain from nasty bruises and cuts on his legs and thighs.

By the time we got him patched up it was close to three o'clock and we were woozy hungry. His wife wanted to feed us. She was from the mainland and had made a bowl of *chiao-tzu,* that delicious, mouth-watering ravioli-like item made from ground pork and vegetables and wrapped in rice dough. It is a mainland favorite. She explained that the next day was some sort of a special religious holiday in the village—each village sets aside days for its own special rites; thus there is no islandwide continuity for many of the holidays—and that was why she had prepared this delicacy.

"The food looks freshly prepared," I said to Maryann in English.

"Well, should we take a chance?" Maryann answered. We had had a few painful experiences with dysentery as the result of eating in other homes and had set up a rule that we would accept no more hospitality. I have noted before about the quick spoilage of food in Taiwan's heat and lack of refrigeration. There was still another matter: sometimes food was prepared the day before, which just compounded the danger of a serious case of dysentery for the Westerner, whose tolerance to this sort of bacteria is very low.

"Gee, I don't know whether to take a chance or not. But I'm hungry as a horse." I was really teetering.

"Her food looks all right, like you said," Maryann sighed, hunger sticking out of every word.

"All right, let's try it. Anyhow, I don't think I could make it back to Talin without something on my stomach."

We piled into that *chiao-tzu* like there was no tomorrow. It was exceptionally delicious, and the farmer's wife had made plenty. So, there was no concern about having to be polite by leaving some in our bowls. With each mouthful we told her nobody ever made *chiao-tzu* like hers. She beamed all over the place and thanked us profusely for honoring her house as we left for Talin. About two hours later, right after we had closed the clinic and were hurrying back to Chiayi, both of us began to feel squeamish.

"My stomach feels funny, crampishlike," Maryann said.

"Mine's not feeling so hot, either." I pressed harder on the accelerator. "In fact, I'll be glad to get back home and take some bismuth."

"I wonder if it was the food," Maryann suggested.

"I've been wondering the same thing. Well, we'll know soon enough." I tried to laugh as though it were a joke.

It was no joke. We wound up with a violent case of dysentery that knocked us out for three days.

We were too sick to leave the convent the next day, but wouldn't you know that we would have patients traipsing out to the mother house? Mother Philomena turned them away, except for a woman with a year-old daughter in her arms. Mother listened to the woman's story (she had come nearly eighty miles by train) and looked at the little girl (she was withered and her lips purple) and her heart melted.

Maryann and I struggled out of bed, put on housecoats and set up a laboratory in the parlor. The child had a temperature of 104 and bacterial diarrhea. She had been sick a month. By now, she was so far gone that she suffered from anemia, malnourishment and also a heart condition. We urged the mother to take the child to a hospital immediately. She shook her head.

"Don't you realize your daughter is very sick, that she might die?" I asked her.

"Yes."

"You must get her to a hospital right away. We can't treat her properly and she needs weeks of constant care." I started to write down the names of some hospitals to give her a broad selection in case she ran into problems.

"I do not have money for a hospital," she said.

Frankly, neither did we. We were on short rations. I suggested that she get in touch with her husband immediately. Perhaps he could send her money once he knew how ill his daughter was. She said she would stay overnight with a relative in Chiayi, and let us know the following day about her husband's decision. She was adamant. Maryann and I did not like this delay, but had no choice in the matter because we had no hospital of our own. We gave her medicine and some infant's powdered milk to get some decent nourishment into the girl.

The mother, all smiles, brought the daughter back to the mother house the next day. "She is better," she smiled.

That part was true enough. The temperature had gone down, and the girl looked a trifle brighter. Maryann set up the laboratory again in the parlor (we were still sick ourselves) and ran another blood count. The hemoglobin count was still a dangerous thirty-five per cent, although the white corpuscle count had gone down a little.

"Your daughter is still very, very sick," I warned the mother. "Have you gotten in touch with your husband?"

She dropped her head. "No." She looked up, eagerly. "But my daughter is getting better."

"Your daughter needs hospital care right now," I stressed. "You get in touch with your husband as soon as you go back to your relatives. Now please don't delay this any longer." I gave her more medicine and powdered milk.

If only we had a hospital, that child would have been in it twenty-four hours before and would have stayed there until she was well again, and at no cost to the parents if they were not able to pay. Yes, if only we had a hospital, that child would be alive today. Instead, she died a few weeks later. The father told his wife to bring the child home; he did not have any money for medical treatment.

Hospital . . . hospital . . . hospital. That word became the most frustrating one in the English language. The little girl was not alone in needless death. There were others, older people, teen-agers, children, infants. There would be more, and our hands were tied.

There were hundreds who did get well, but their recovery was long, and, in some cases, meant loss of their jobs because we had only out-patient clinic care to offer at a time when they needed a hospital bed and hospital care. Thomas Chow was one of these. He was forty years old. Because of a congenital deformity of the arms, he was lost in the shuffle among the healthy ones in his family and ended up doing odd jobs, barely earning a living. A priest in Thomas Chow's town told us that the man had started wasting away because of tropical ulcers all over his legs. Could we do something? We brought him by ambulance to Chiayi. He stayed with friends not far from the mother house. We began treatment with medicines and ointments, and each day on the way home from a clinic trip we stopped off to change the dressing.

He began to respond nicely, then had a relapse. It developed that Thomas decided he was well enough to skip the ointment applications and would be out roaming the streets when we came by. We tried light dosages of penicillin, and he responded. He had to stay under our care for nearly six months before he was well enough to return home. In the meantime, the people he had worked for decided they could not wait any longer for him and found others to do their odd jobs. Thus, Thomas Chow was reduced to begging. If we had only had a hospital, he would have been on his feet in three weeks, four at the most. He would not have become a beggar. That is another reason the word "hospital" became such a frustrating thing.

I cannot forget either a three-year-old girl who had a mild case of polio in her legs. We got her over the hump and showed the mother passive exercises that eventually would permit her daughter to walk again. She made slow but steady progress in that direction, reaching the stage where she could stand alone. But the parents became impatient over the slow improvement. They heard of a "quack" who was supposed to be good at speedy recovery. He used his fingernails to cut into the skin and bring blood into the legs. His treatment failed, naturally. Now the girl cannot even stand, but must crawl along the floor. Moreover, she never will be able to stand or walk.

Such were the heartbreaking things; such were some of the cases that put us in a position of just struggling along, doing the best we could with the limited facilities of out-patient clinics. Would we always have to struggle this way, or would we be able to make greater progress through a hospital? I mean simply this: the opportunity for the Our Lady of China community to branch out with vocations in the fields of medicine. The end result would provide improved health benefits for the people and bring Christ's love to more people.

We had then a pre-medical student among our novices (she is now in Italy finishing her medical training) who will become our first sister surgeon. We also had young girls among the aspirants and postulants who wanted to train in nursing but had no qualified place to learn the profession. And we had Sister Catherine Chang back with us. Doing X-ray work, in which she had taken her degree in the United States? No. She was a novice mistress. You see, we had no X-ray department. While Sister Catherine was doing excellent work with the novices, her skill as an X-ray technician was being wasted.

How could we overcome this no-hospital handicap? Why, with money, of course. How much? About $35,000 for a fifty-bed hospital and second-hand X ray, and another $15,-000 for beds, night tables, operating-room equipment, laboratory, pharmacy and so forth. Those were estimates we obtained from an architect who drew up plans for a hospital in 1963. Some place in this world there just had to be enough people willing to help us. My eyes turned eastward, toward the United States. Our mother house came from there. Perhaps a hospital would, too. I was due for home leave in the fall of 1964. It was agreed within the community that Sister Raphael would be my traveling companion and that we would spend a few months in fund raising and public relations. The latter item was prompted by only nineteen replies from our 1963 Christmas letter to a mailing list of 350 people. We had to rejuvenate interest in the

Sisters of Our Lady of China and make many, many more contacts to build a solid foundation of Americans of good will. Our agenda also included finding an American-trained doctor, and also another nurse to replace Maryann, whose two-year stay with us would expire shortly before Sister Raphael and I left for the States.

In looking back, I sometimes wonder how I ever got out of Taiwan in one piece. Everything just seemed to go haywire at one time: a strange retreat, an off-schedule passenger-freighter, and a typhoon. We closed down our clinic work the first week in October. Maryann and one of the nuns, Sister Theresa Duh-li, began stowing hundreds of bottles of medicines in gunny sacks. They would go down to the clinic early in the morning while I cleaned up a few chores at the mother house. As soon as I walked into the clinic, somebody would rush down the street and pretty soon there would be a group pleading, "Please, just me," or "That medicine you gave me did so much good; I need more." And there we were, going out of our minds rooting through the sacks and trying to find the right bottles.

After we had cleaned out the clinic and retired to the mother house, the patients got our address and began rushing out there. Every day there would be a couple of dozen patients. Meantime, I was preparing for a week's retreat. Things got so bad that I had to go to another convent in Chiayi. Even so, there was no relief, since the grapevine spread the word. I finally returned to the mother house to begin the retreat. It went out of kilter right from the start. On the first day, the priest who was giving me my retreat collapsed on his way to visit the Furen High School operated by the S.V.D. order. The word we received at the convent was that he was dying right out in the middle of the street. Mother Philomena pulled me out of retreat, and I went whizzing over in the ambulance. He was all right. He had collapsed from heat exhaustion. Then, another priest came out to the mother house for treatment. He had hives from head to foot and felt miserable.

Another day, a mother brought a little boy who had been a patient of ours. He had chronic nephritis and had been fine for about two years. All of a sudden, boom! there was a flareup. The mother came out to the convent every day and pleaded at the gate. Naturally, we took care of her son. A man angrily pounded on the gate when a sister tried to turn him away. His son had pneumonia and the father insisted that I was the only person who could cure him. A priest at Furen High School came down with pneumonia, too, and that meant daily trips to his bedside. The retreat was just a mess.

The day the retreat ended there was only a week left before the boat sailed for California. I had planned to use that time in finishing up all my affairs, such as book work on cases and medications, paying bills, having the ambulance put up on blocks, getting clothing ready and packed, and a zillion and one little things. A telegram arrived from the steamship line: the boat was ahead of schedule and would sail in forty-eight hours. At almost the same time the wire arrived, a government official, whose wife had had a stroke and was relieved with our medications, came charging out to the mother house and expressed unhappiness about our trip.

"You cannot go away," he said, flatfootedly. "You are the only ones who have been successful in treating her. You have to stay."

By this time, my head was spinning.

There were some social obligations, too. An X-ray technician and a laboratory technician who did work for our clinics insisted on giving a bon voyage party. As painfully cramped as we were for time (we were leaving for Keelung and the boat the next morning), it was simply impossible to turn them down. They would have lost face.

"I cannot understand why you must go to America to raise money," the X-ray man said during dinner.

"That is not the way to do it," the laboratory technician said. "You are taking all that time away from your work here. It is not necessary."

"All right, how would you do it?" I inquired.

They were amazed. "You do not know how?"

"Well, I don't know what you have in mind."

They smiled, looked at each other, and finally the laboratory man supplied the secret. "It is perfectly simple. All you have to do is write a letter to Rome or a few people in America. You will receive all the money you will ever need."

America, the fabled land of the gold apple trees!

Some of the sisters themselves had similar notions. As we waited at the railroad station the next morning—dead tired from about only two hours sleep after staying up most of the night packing clothing, a few thousand pieces of literature about our work, and other odds and ends—they assured us we would be back in two or three months.

"The boat trip takes over a month round trip," I said.

"Oh, we know that," one answered with a flick of her hand. "You will spend a month with your family, see a few people about the hospital, and that is all there is to it."

It sounded all so simple that I was beginning to believe them. Sister Raphael and I boarded the train for Taipei in high spirits. If we could have foreseen the future, maybe we would not have looked forward to that trip with such light hearts.

CHAPTER TWELVE

As we rode the bus from Taipei to Keelung, my thoughts took a fleeting turn backward. It was nearly five years since I had made this same ocean voyage, but in reverse. Much had happened, far more than I had ever dreamed in that relatively short span. And now, it was back to the United States for an in-person project to stimulate interest in and more progress for the Our Lady of China community.

"It will be wonderful if everything works out as well as everybody believes," I said.

Sister Raphael smiled. "We will have no problems."

"I really hope not, but offhand I can't think of anything that could go wrong. Anyhow, it will be nice to have a chance for a restful sea voyage before we go back to work." I settled back in the seat, closed my eyes, and thought of all the sleep I would get on the freighter, and the quiet, peaceful days sunning on the deck.

A few hours later, with the boat barely out of the harbor, things started to go kaput. A typhoon was boiling up. Big, strong swells developed, and the freighter started rocking. As we finished dinner, Sister Raphael turned green, hurriedly excused herself and started out of the dining room. She never made it to the door; she was sick as a pup. Although the captain skirted the center of the storm, the boat pitched and tossed, sometimes at a forty-five-degree angle, for days on end. It was impossible to walk without being thrown against bulkheads, and sleep was at a premium. We lost four days in the crossing. The eighteen-day voyage turned into twenty days. But it was just the beginning of a worry-fraught, sad journey that would not end for a year.

We docked at San Pedro, California, in mid-afternoon of November 12, 1964. Everything seemed so strange—nothing but Americans everywhere. Harold Anderson's sister, Mrs. Patricia Thirkill of Whittier, California, met us and drove us to the Los Angeles airport to catch a plane for a reunion with Pop, Jo, and my brother Bill and his family in Sacramento. As we drove from San Pedro, my eyes kept popping and so did Sister Raphael's. Huge skyscrapers, mile after mile of one- and two-family houses, highways jammed with autos, the splendor of the people's clothing (everybody looked so spruced up), towering oil derricks. It seemed that every American had the key to Fort Knox. Sister Raphael who had never been in the United States, was even more impressed by this vast panorama of wealth. The bon voyage words we had heard in Chiayi—"We will look for you in a few months"—came back to us. Why, we had our hospital money in the bag; maybe right here on the West Coast. After five years in Taiwan and now all of a sudden transported into a golden fairyland, I, too, looked at the United States through the eyes of a foreigner.

It was exciting to be with the family again, although I did shock Jo and Pop. I had picked up a sound, "eh," used in Taiwanese to emphasize a point, and unconsciously injected it into my English conversation. My parents lost no time at all in trying to break me of that habit. "Are you deaf?" they would ask, repeatedly, as the word did sound something like the one used by elderly people with a hearing problem.

The family reunion did have one disturbing element. I learned that Bill had cancer. When Sister Raphael and I began our fund-raising journey a week later, it would be the last time I would see Bill. I was not aware of this, since Bill had assured everybody that the cancer had been arrested. Only his wife, Phyl, knew the true story and she tactfully spared us in order that the all-too-brief get-together would not turn into a semi-wake.

We were anxious to reach Seattle because it would be our first chance to meet Mr. Anderson. He was a human dynamo as our mission promoter in the United States. He was in his late twenties, lean, tall and loose-gaited. He and his wife and three children and his mother made us feel at home right away. It was as though we had been life-long, personal friends rather than pen pals, so to speak, for about three years. We had planned only two days in Seattle to go over our itinerary, hoping that Mr. Anderson would have some suggestions, and also pick up the half-fare passes the American railroads had issued to us and forwarded to his office at 1001 East Pike Street. Moreover, we wanted to give the Anderson family a message—the hospital would be named in honor of Mr. Anderson's father, Martin, who had been killed in a traffic accident a short time before. Martin Anderson, who was not a Catholic, exemplified the ecumenical spirit. He made personal contributions to our work, and enlisted many of his friends in helping us financially. In selecting a saint with his name for the hospital, our community chose St. Martin de Porres, a Dominican lay brother who had spent a lifetime working with the sick and beggars in Peru.

The two days stretched into a week. Mr. Anderson had taken time away from his duties as head of the Northwest Trophy Company, which was founded by his father, to line up a series of meetings at which we would tell our story and show color slides of our work with the sick. Sister Raphael and I had not actually planned to start the lectures until we reached Chicago a few weeks later. We figured on speaking in the Seattle area on the way back to Taiwan. As a result of Mr. Anderson's early groundwork, Sister and I hurriedly put together notes for a half-hour, illustrated lecture.

"What can we talk about?" I asked Sister Raphael. There were butterflies in my stomach, like stage fright. We knew our work inside and out. But now, to tell about it, the whole picture turned into a mish-mash. The lecture platform suddenly became an ogre.

"You will talk about some of the patients, of course," Sister Raphael suggested. "Why they come to your clinics, how they feel about us, what happened to them."

My mind was still just a blur of hundreds of faces flying about and suddenly not able to identify any one of them. It was a frightening thing, and I was already beginning to worry about getting up on the platform. "Do you have anybody particular in mind?"

"There is Ah-na."

"Ah-na," I broke in. "Yes, oh, yes." I felt relieved, for here at least was one person to be pulled out of the blur of faces. There really is no Chinese name like that; it was the English Anna to which we had given a Chinese pronunciation for some reason that I cannot recall. Anyhow, Ah-na was a little mountain girl who had collapsed on the street after school in Mei-shan. She was on her way to catch a bus home. She had appendicitis. An old man picked her up and brought her to the clinic. When I asked him why he chose us, he answered, "Everybody knows that you will take good care of her and find her parents. I have no money to help her, but all the people know you care for the sick and helpless without cost."

"Can you think of any more?" I asked Sister.

"Would you like to talk about some of the ways people without money pay for treatment? I can think of the three little sisters you called 'The Marias' and the Christmas tree."

"Sure," I chuckled, feeling more and more comfortable about putting together the lecture notes. I never could keep their names straight. That is why I called them all Maria. "You remember how the mother was always bringing one or another to the clinic—and each time it was pneumonia? I still don't understand how they ever survived so many bouts with pneumonia, but they did. It surely had to be all that good medicine from the United States."

The Marias' family could not afford to pay us anything. In some cases, the poor voluntarily gave us some rice, eggs, or sweet potatoes as token payments, but The Marias' father did something different to show his appreciation. He made an artificial Christmas tree that we put up every year at the mother house. Every bit of it is bamboo—the trunk, branches and even the needles, which he delicately cut into strips not much thicker than strands of hair and worked into tufts of "pine" needles. It is the most beautiful, artificial Christmas tree I have ever seen. It looks so natural that some visitors have gone away insisting that it is a real pine tree.

"Do you want to talk about Pao-p'ei?" Sister Raphael asked.

Pao-p'ei, Precious One. His name, his illness saddened me. My mind wandered back a year. He was a splendid example of what a hospital could mean. We gave him his nickname the day his uncle carried him piggy-back into the Chiayi clinic. He was twelve years old and had one of the sweetest faces and dispositions imaginable. His parents were farmers, but he lived with an uncle across the street from the clinic while he attended school in the city. Pao-p'ei had aplastic anemia. It is usually fatal, although cures have been effected. I recalled how Maryann and I did a blood work-up that showed a hemoglobin count of only twenty-two per cent. He needed hospitalization, but there was no hospital that could spare a bed. When he did not respond to anti-anemia medication, we switched to blood transfusions from willing donors. This did not seem to help, and we turned to liver, iron, vitamin B-12, and corticoid. Our Precious One responded and we were overjoyed.

"Oh, if we could only have a hospital, give him the best medical care, watch him day and night—I know he would get well," I often said to Maryann.

Pao-p'ei took a turn for the worse, and we talked to a Western-trained physician, who recommended a splenectomy. After the operation, we kept him on medication and Precious One picked up beautifully. His hemoglobin count went up to fifty-seven per cent; we were witnessing a remarkable recovery. But Pao-p'ei became homesick and went home to his parents, against our advice. While at home, he caught a cold and had a relapse. He failed to respond to further treatment.

Precious One started asking questions about God and Jesus, and loved to hear Biblical stories. A priest visited his home and Pao-p'ei's parents, a Buddhist family, gave permission for him to be baptized. A few days later, the priest stopped by the house and found Precious One slipping rapidly, but talking about God and Jesus. He died an hour later with a smile on his face. I have always been convinced that if we had had a hospital, Precious One would be alive today.

The stories of Ah-na, The Marias and Pao-p'ei impressed our audiences, and we took off a week later from Seattle confident that we did have a story to tell and that the American people wanted to hear it.

The weather was balmy as the train pulled out for the East. A few hours later, going through the fir-clad Cascades, it started to snow. It snowed practically all the way to Bismarck and our appointment with Sister Mary Paul, the administrator of St. Alexius Hospital and a friend of our Sister Catherine Chang. We wanted to thank her and the

Benedictine Sisters for the huge amount of clothing, blankets, medical supplies and medication they had so generously sent to us. Also, we wanted to go over our hospital's plans with Sister Paul. We were certain that she could give us some ideas. She did—and something else: a snazzy sports car.

Her warm office was quite a contrast to the weather outside, snow and thirty degrees below zero. "It's a little different here than in Taiwan," she laughed. With that, there was a rap on the door and a physician came in. He said he was getting a new sports car and wanted to donate his old one, a 1960 Corvette, to the Benedictine Sisters.

Oh, boy, I thought, wouldn't that be something if he had given it to us.

Sister Paul looked at Sister Raphael and me, excused herself and then rushed out of the office with the doctor in tow. She returned a few minutes later, all smiles. "Well, Sisters, no more public transportation for you. You have a car."

It was so unbelievable, as if the whole thing had been pre-arranged. We were walking—rather, riding—on air, and headed through a series of snowstorms and sub-zero weather for a reunion with Maryann in Dubuque. It was actually more than that. We wanted Maryann to line up lectures for us during January after Sister Raphael and I had returned from a vacation with Pop and Jo in Largo, Florida. Before going South, we went to Chicago and saw Mrs. Wall, our Midwestern dynamo, and some other friends about setting up some January fund-raising appearances. We left the car in Chicago and took a train to Florida.

Our spirits were not very good. We had been in the United States over a month and had not even begun to make a dent in our goal of $35,000 for the hospital building fund. In nearly a dozen lectures we had given thus far, there had been no hundred dollar bills in the collection plates. Mostly ones and silver.

"This is not going to be a three to four month thing," I said to Sister Raphael as the train carried us toward the Southland.

"No," she said. "It is not going to be as easy as we had thought."

"Let's go back to Chicago the first week in January," I suggested. "We'll take care of immediate engagements and try to set up a two-month lecture tour of Michigan, Illinois, Wisconsin and Iowa starting in April, and, in the meantime, go East." This plan meant cutting our Florida vacation short, but I was worried. Sister Raphael nodded agreement.

"Maybe we'll be able to start back to the West Coast around the middle of June and be on our way home in early July." Even when I said it, my fingers were crossed.

We had planned to stay in Florida three full weeks, but at the end of the second week we decided to return to Chicago and resume our work. But we had not counted on the heavy tourist traffic at that time of the year. Thus, there was no space available on a train, bus or plane for nearly two weeks. That put a real crimp in our schedule. Meantime, the stay in Florida developed into a working vacation. There was lots of correspondence about lecture dates, letters to people who had made private contributions, and talks before the Lions Club of Largo and some church groups. We spoke before the congregation at the Anona Community Methodist Church, of which my father is treasurer. Father Roman Gromala, pastor of my stepmother's church, St. Jerome's, arranged for meetings with different members of the parish and an opportunity to show slides of our work in Taiwan.

Our activities became the subject of a newspaper article in Largo. As a result of the story, we received a telephone call from a ninety-two-year-old woman, Mrs. Anna Gullage, who, along with her husband and several children, had spent a lifetime of service with the Salvation Army. I single out Mrs. Gullage for one reason: she was the zenith of charity and ecumenical living.

Mrs. Gullage apologized over the phone that, because of infirmities, she was unable to come to us, but would we visit her? She wanted to contribute a dollar. Her thoughtfulness was genuine. Still, I had a feeling that she needed the dollar more than we did, and hedged as politely as possible about setting a time to see her. A few days later, she phoned again. "Where have you been?" She was upset.

Mrs. Gullage gave us ten one-dollar bills. Despite the problems she had in getting around, she visited neighbors to borrow the money to add to her dollar. Nobody could match that for living by the Golden Rule.

When Sister Raphael and I returned to Chicago in the forepart of January, it was as though we had never left Florida. The temperature was seventy degrees. Within twenty-four hours, the tropical mirage was gone. The temperature plunged, snow arrived, and our work just about became snowbound in one of the worst winters the Midwest had had in a generation. No matter what we planned it went haywire. We drove up to Kalamazoo to see Father Kuo, who was teaching then at Nazareth College. A snowstorm hit. We were twenty-four hours late in getting back to Chicago, and two lecture dates went down the drain. We started for Dubuque one Sunday evening so that we would get a good night's sleep prior to a speaking engagement at a high school the next morning. We had hardly left Chicago when an ice storm came up, and cars began skidding and even turning over. I looked for a motel but other motorists had been doing the same thing. We did not find a vacancy until two o'clock in the morning. The roads were still treacherous when we got up, and we arrived half-way through the assembly programs. By then, Sister Raphael and I were a couple of nervous wrecks.

Our weather woes were far from being over. A sleet storm knocked out a tea of sixty influential ladies in Evanston, Illinois. My former teachers among the Ursuline Sisters invited us to Decatur. I stepped out of the car in front of the convent. The street was absolutely dry except for a small icy spot that I did not see. I slipped, fell heavily, and wound up at a hospital with a possible fractured knee. Fortunately, the X rays were negative, but the knee was puffed out and painful for days. Shortly thereafter, we had a morning appointment with an important clergyman in Milwaukee. When we left Chicago, I was running a temperature. On top of that, a blinding snowstorm developed on the way. We never did get to see him.

All was not lost, though, in Milwaukee. Mrs. James Enslow helped in contacting quite a few schools and mission groups for fund-raising talks and arranged for an article in the diocesan paper. We stayed at Cardinal Stritch College, which is operated by the Sisters of St. Francis of Assisi. One of the nuns said, "While you are here, you must go and see some of our Chinese sisters."

We drove crosstown, thinking it would be like back home for a little while, sitting around and talking with the Chinese nuns again. Lo and behold, it was a joyful reunion. There were nuns Sister Raphael had not seen since her days in mainland China. And one in particular, Sister Claudia. She had been Sister Raphael's math teacher when sister was an aspirant in Shantung.

We were not collecting much money, but, for a short time at least, we were enjoying a delightful respite from fund raising and the concern it was causing us. There was also concern over Sister Raphael. She had not seemed her old, jolly self. She had developed a cough and sore throat. A doctor in Chicago said it was bronchitis, and, most likely, a touch of homesickness.

An experience in a Chicago department store did not help the latter. We had gone shopping for a new projector screen and were heading for the exit. I thought Sister was right behind me. Instead, at the door, she was nowhere in sight. I looked every which way, but no Sister Raphael. After a while, I heard a woman's shrill voice. "Don't let them do it! Don't let them do it! "A crowd was gathering, and, in between bobbing heads, I saw Sister Raphael. She was white as a ghost. The woman had her by the shoulders and pinned against a counter.

"What's wrong?" I demanded, shoving through the crowd.

The woman turned abruptly to me. "Don't let them do it!"

"Do what?" I asked while shouldering up to Sister Raphael's side.

"Change the style of your habits! That's what!!"

I breathed a big sigh of relief. It was around the time the first stories appeared about modernizing nun's habits. This woman was from the old school. Still, this was not the time and place to start a public debate, although I could have told her an ankle-length habit, a starched collar and a headdress were uncomfortable in sub-tropical climates; that the hems became dirty quickly from the dusty roads during the dry season and muddy in the rainy periods. I had thought for some time there should be modifications— not the high school girl extremes, as some designers had suggested—to make the habit more comfortable.

"We'll do the best we can," I assured the woman, took Sister Raphael by the arm and led her from the store. I tried to make a joke of the whole thing, but sister was not quite up to it.

In spite of that unnerving incident for Sister Raphael, Chicago treated us warmly. Mrs. Wall and her friend, Mrs.

Mary Bernero, pitched in, as did many others to try to make our trip a success.

For the time being, though, we had gone about as far as we could on our fund raising in the Midwest. Our spring lecture tour was set up; we got a dandy trade-in on the Corvette for a Volkswagen sedan (the sports car was beginning to give us some oil and gas problems); and we made some contacts in Ohio and on the East Coast through friends in the Midwest. On the way East, we made a few stops and finally arrived in Trenton, New Jersey, on what quickly turned into a discouraging meandering to Philadelphia and Washington. Trenton said, "You had better see so-and-so in Philadelphia." Philadelphia said, "Your best bet is such-and-such in Washington." Washington said, "You would save a lot of time if you see Bishop Sheen in New York. I will make an appointment."

We were down in the dumps. Almost a week of wandering in the East and hardly a nickle to show for it. The $35,000 seemed like an impossibility. Okay, let's go see the Most Reverend Fulton J. Sheen. As director of the Propagation of the Faith in the United States, he might have some ideas.

Bishop Sheen was wonderful! He sat with us for over a half hour, listening to our tale of woe. When we left him, I can say that we were no longer two disheartened nuns. He gave us some excellent suggestions and also urged us to make an appointment with Catholic Relief Services-N.C.W.C., as had a Benedictine priest, Father Alvin Herbel, who gave us a contact there. Bishop Sheen was the turning point in our trip. Or was it really Trenton? If we had not gone there in the first place and followed the discouraging trail to Washington, we never would have seen Bishop Sheen. It was as though God were testing our faith.

We arrived at Catholic Relief Services in the Empire State Building in a state of awe. It was a bustling place. Here we were, just a couple of begging nuns from a little community tucked away in a small corner of Taiwan. We looked out a window sixty-five stories above the ground and saw the hugeness of New York City sprawling out below us. That made us feel even more insignificant. What a lot of crust we have in bothering these people, I thought. Sure, Catholic Relief Services representatives in Taipei had been very helpful, but that was in Taiwan and they knew us. But here we were in the international headquarters of the largest voluntary overseas aid agency in the United States through which flowed thousands of appeals for food, clothing and medicines each year.

The reception we received quickly changed our minds that we were small potatoes. Mathia Marley, who was then supervisor of the Far East desk, made us feel like old friends. She knew about us, and displayed a keen interest in our work and our hospital plans. She suggested that we draw up a detailed project report, even down to the cost of a night light, and submit it along with blueprints of the hospital. Miss Marley also arranged for us to meet with the Right Reverend Joseph J. Harnett, the C.R.S. director for Asia and the Far East who was in New York at the time. Monsignor Harnett treated us royally and went out of his way to be helpful.

Sister Raphael and I walked light-headed and light-footed crosstown to the Leo House—a Benedictine priest had paid for two weeks' lodgings—and plunged into drawing up the project report. We had hardly started when I received a long distance call that my brother Bill was dying. His death came nearly four months to the day we had said good-by in mid-November. The news knocked the starch out of us. I remember Sister Raphael comforting me and telling me not to cry. Little did either of us know that three weeks later she would be going into a hospital because of cancer.

By the time the report was finished, Sister Raphael and

I had moved to the St. Jerome's Convent of the Ursuline Sisters in the Bronx. One evening, when our fund raising seemed to have come to a complete standstill again, I said to the sisters, "The Ursulines got me into this. Now how about the Ursulines helping to bail me out." Although I was laughing, the superior, Mother Ignatius, took me seriously.

"Sister Paul, what have we done wrong?"

"Why, you know that I became a Catholic because of the Ursulines being 'God's instrument'—St. Teresa's Academy—Mother Paul Ketter." Everybody was laughing now.

"I don't see any reason why we should not try to help build that hospital," Mother Mary Roberts said. She went on to point out that she was a friend of a key figure in one of the leading foundations in the United States.

"Somebody has already contacted that organization," I said.

"I don't see any harm in my writing, too, do you?" The end result was an appointment with Mother Mary Roberts' friend. But we left, after a pleasant visit, without a firm commitment.

I think it was the next day, at dinner, that Sister Raphael's persistent sore throat and coughing gave a broad hint of something more serious than we had believed. She had eaten some carrots and peas without difficulty, but a piece of meat stuck in her throat momentarily before being vomited back up.

A few days later, Sister Raphael was in Misericordia Hospital in the Bronx. She had cancer of the esophagus. Her chances of recovery were regarded as poor. First my brother Bill, and now Sister Raphael. I cannot think of any period in my life when my spirits were so low. It just seemed that ill fortune was dogging both of us. And now with Sister very, very sick, it appeared that our hospital fund-raising trip was doomed. True, we had received much encouragement from many people, but a lot of it was moral support. At that particular time, however, discouragement was the keynote of our efforts. Even some of the people we had met were hostile. They berated us, asserting, "You are trying to collect money for the Chinese who are the main reason for the war in Vietnam and killing our boys." Those people were totally unaware that there are two Chinas, the Communist government on the mainland responsible for the wars in Asia, and the Chinese in Taiwan who stand four-square as our friends and allies in the struggle for freedom in the Orient. Although these ill-informed individuals were a small minority, it seemed that now, in this dark hour, that there antipathy overshadowed the eagerly given and generous help of all kinds provided by the great majority of Americans we had met. My mind was involved in one of those cruel psychological quirks so typical of times of stress.

The money we had collected thus far, less than $10,000 in four months of eighteen-hours-a-day, hard-nosed fund raising, became a question mark for us as our hospital nest egg. We had no hospitalization or medical insurance of any kind, and I was well aware of the tremendous expense attendant to the treatment of cancer. Although Sister Raphael was not told she had cancer, she guessed it nonetheless. She would have to stay in the hospital six weeks for cobalt therapy. That meant, of course, that our two-month tour of the Midwest, scheduled to start in a few weeks, had to be canceled. I privately debated whether it would be worthwhile staying in the States or packing up immediately and flying Sister Raphael back to Taipei for admission to one of the fine hospitals there. It would have meant, naturally, giving up our hospital goal, or at least delaying it for a few years. I was not only in a quandary about that but also in a state of depression. I prayed long hours for guidance, and it always seemed that I was told to wait, to continue on, not to give up.

Sister Marcelle, the administrator at Misericordia Hospital, assured and reassured us not to worry one moment about hospital expenses of any kind. Sister Raphael was given a private room while the X-ray department began the lengthy cobalt therapy. The Sisters of St. Francis of Assisi in Milwaukee sent Sister Claudia to help care for Sister Raphael. The cobalt therapy stopped the cancer's spread and an operation was recommended. It was then that I was given the depressing task of telling sister that she had to have surgery.

She said six words: "When do they want to operate?" Her bravery was something to behold. There she was, skin and bones and very sick. I sensed that she knew her chances were slim—actually a paper-thin five per cent. But never once did she shed a tear, or utter a hopeless or sad thought. She prayed; all of us prayed—the Ursuline Sisters, the Sisters of Misericordia, and countless other people we had come to know. If anybody can attest to the power and greatness of prayer, we can.

The chief surgeon at Misericordia Hospital, Dr. Benedict M. Reynolds, and a thorasic surgeon, Dr. Andrew T. Manuele, took over the case. Drs. Manuele and Reynolds operated on Sister Raphael in June of 1965 and performed a one-stage removal of the esophagus and a colon transplant. It was an eight-hour-plus operation. Within a few days, Sister Raphael was up and smiling. Her chances of recovery were smiling, too.

But that was not all the good news. Dr. Reynolds' wife arranged for a hospital fund collection for us in the parish school. Dr. Reynolds and Dr. Manuele themselves gave generously to the fund. A bill? It was unthinkable.

Even while the cobalt therapy was under way, Sister Raphael and I turned her room into somewhat of an office to continue our work. Every day there would be a stack of mail, the bulk of it get-well cards. Here and there was a check for a dollar or so for the fund. And then came a letter from Catholic Relief Services-N.C.W.C. It reported a substantial contribution by Mr. Romy Hammes of Kankakee, Illinois, to C.R.S. in memory of his deceased wife Dorothy. Following right on its heels was a letter from Mother Mary Roberts' foundation friend with another substantial check. We were starting to see daylight! We needed only to pull a few more financial clouds away to assure the Sisters of Our Lady of China of a hospital in Chiayi City. So, it was back to the campaign trail while Sister continued with the cobalt therapy.

The first stop was Cincinnati and Mr. and Mrs. Wesley Ungerbuehler, who had made dozens and dozens of phone calls in our behalf. A Chicago relative of the Ungerbuehlers had given us their name. Sister Raphael and I had visited them on our way East. They and their five children—one an adopted Chinese girl, whose name was Maria, by the way—welcomed us with open arms. The Ungerbuehlers set up an extensive lecture series for us in the Cincinnati area. It was to precede immediately the spring talks we had scheduled in Illinois, Wisconsin, Iowa and Michigan. And now, while Sister was in the hospital, I returned to carry out at least part of the series they had worked up.

Back in New York, and right before Sister underwent surgery, I mapped a trip through New Jersey, New York and Pennsylvania as far West as Erie, followed immediately by one to Connecticut, Rhode Island and Massachusetts. Sister Claudia went along. The two trips were a complete bust. We covered 4,000 miles and grossed ten dollars. It was not even enough to put a dent in the highway tolls, let alone gas, oil and garage bills, and the cost of food while we were on the road. Sister Claudia and I were really downhearted by the time we stopped off in Bridgeport, Con-

necticut, on our return to New York City. We had hoped to
see the Right Reverend David Bannon, but he was out of
town. While we chatted with his secretary, Mrs. Phyllis Hes-
sels, it turned out that she was a convert, too. We developed
a rapport, and, as Sister Claudia and I were leaving, she
said, 'Keep in touch with us. The monsignor is having a
Propagation of the Faith collection. Maybe something can
be worked out." Thus a casual conversation resulted in a
church being assigned and a nice check.

And then I wound up in the raffle business. A friend
made the suggestion and donated the raffle books. His
Knights of Columbus chapter was the sponsor. If there is
any reader of this book who remembers me sitting in the
fourth floor solarium at Misericordia Hospital in July, 1965,
typing up lists of names, it was for the raffle. But I had
help from Mrs. Yolanda Gorassi, who literally broke a foot
for me. She was president of the Women's Guild of the
Our Lady of Grace Church in the Bronx. She had a heart
as big as the world, and a family just like her, and scads of
loyal friends. She supplied lists of potential raffle buyers
and also helped get rid of the books. The raffle went off
just fine. We added $750 to our hospital building fund.

Mrs. Gorassi came into our lives in a roundabout way.
Shortly before we left Chicago, Mrs. Wall asked us to look
up Monsignor Heinrich Rumph, the head of the St. Boniface
Society in the Bronx. Until we met Bishop Sheen, Monsignor
Rumph was our only contact in New York, but I did not
have an opportunity to see him until Sister Raphael's illness.
He was very gracious, arranged for a contribution, and had
us meet Monsignor John B. Rettagliata of Our Lady of
Grace. He invited us to lunch, and there was much reminiscing, since he had spent twenty years in the Army, much
of it in Asia. He also arranged for us to speak to some of the
church's groups, among them the Women's Guild. Enter
Mrs. Gorassi.

While Sister Raphael was in the hospital, Mrs. Gorassi or one of her relatives never failed to pay a daily visit and also bring along all sorts of tempting dishes to whet sister's poor appetite. Even a broken foot did not stop her from the hospital visits. The break happened in the strangest of ways. She got up on a chair to go through some boxes on a closet shelf for a hat to wear to a reception for Archbishop Yupin. She and I had been invited to the affair at Gracie Mansion (the home of New York City's mayors). The chair slipped and she broke her foot in the fall.

When Sister Raphael was ready to come out of the hospital, Mrs. Gorassi had a plan ready. Sister would stay at her house during the day while I went about the business of raising funds and arranging for medical equipment and medicines for our clinics and forthcoming hospital. She solved a problem that had been nagging me for weeks. There never was a problem in the hospital. Sister Fernand, the fourth floor supervisor, always made certain Sister was taken care of while I was out. (Sister Claudia had returned to Milwaukee.) As for sleeping accommodations, we had a choice of returning to the St. Jerome's parish of the Ursuline Sisters, with whom we had stayed before sister's illness, or going to the Susan Devin Home in the Bronx at the invitation of Sister M. Josetta, the superior, and the Sisters of Charity. We decided on the Susan Devin Home. It was only a short distance from the Gorassi's, thus making the daily trips easier on Sister Raphael.

Mid-August came and Sister Raphael was well enough to start back to the West Coast and then on home to Chiayi City a month later after I made fund-raising stops in a few cities across the country. Although we both were anxious to get home, it was very hard saying good-by to all the wonderful friends we had made in the Bronx. This was our second home; we stayed there longer—nearly five months—than any other place in the United States. Still, we had to leave; there was work yet to be finished; and it was important that Sister Raphael go home among her other friends she longed to see. Because she was not up to cross-country motoring, she flew to Seattle to stay with the Harold Andersons while I drove. I made some stops that included arranging for medical supplies and equipment, some of which were shipped to the West Coast docks through the charity of the Consolidated Freight Lines.

When we arrived in the United States, nearly a year before, we had planned to contact many diocesan offices of the Propagation of the Faith. Those plans, like so many others, had to be curtailed because of Sister's illness. As a result, our contacts were limited to offices in Chicago, Bridgeport, Indianapolis, Brooklyn, Cincinnati, Pittsburgh, Philadelphia, New York, and Fall River and Springfield, Massachusetts. In every one of them, we were received most warmly.

By the time Sister and I were reunited in Seattle, we had enough money for our hospital building, thanks to the generous hearts of so many American people and organizations. Their generosity will not be forgotten in Taiwan. The story of their help will always be a part of the hospital's story to the Chinese people. It will be a part of the story told to the hospital's patients and to the young people in the high school and orphanage we hope to build in the future.

All of us in the Sisters of Our Lady of China are grateful for what America has done for us. I am grateful also to the sisters themselves and to the Chinese people as a whole in Taiwan, since they have done much for me by making my life fuller and richer than I had ever dreamed it would be. Often they and I forget that we come from different parts of the world. Our color is different; our facial structure is different; many of the customs are different. Yet, as we work together in one family, we forget that we are from different parts of the world; we forget that we do not look alike. I feel that they are like me; they feel I am just like them. When I went to Taiwan, I wanted to be like the Chinese, do what they did, and be one among them. I did not want to be pointed out as somebody different, or given preferential treatment.

Kipling said that the East is East and the West is West and never the twain shall meet. I think that is fast being proven wrong. I also think that if we know each other better, if there is more togetherness, we will not war against each other. There are Americans who say that is impossible; that you can never be one among other people. Many of them do not even try for that one reason. Sister Raphael and I have heard this in Taiwan and the United States, much to our dismay.

I believe that I have made a point that togetherness is possible. The two Western-born nuns in Taipei—Sisters Luke and Chow of the Little Sisters of St. Teresa—have the same feeling I have. When the Japanese came into China and pulled these sisters out of their Chinese community, all of the other sisters said "How come you are taking them away and not taking us?" The Chinese sisters had forgotten they were different from the Western sisters, Luke and Chow.

In my own community, the Sisters of Our Lady of China, we are blended as a family. I went to them as a stranger, an Occidental among Orientals. They welcomed me; they made me feel at home. I will always cherish their kindnesses and thoughtfulness, and for giving me the name of *Hua Shufang*, China's Virtuous Beauty.

A missionary has two interrelated functions—to love God and man. That theme is in the triangle of the Mystical Body of Christ: God, the people and you. It is not just God and you, or you and the people. It is all three linked together, working to help one another. In their zeal, some may relegate that thesis to a secondary role. They may go abroad with the idea that they are going to revolutionize people's lives. Or they are lured by the romance of a huge, tropical moon bathing flower-lined jungle paths and strips of warm, sandy beaches in silvery light. Or they are seeking to escape a problem back home and expect to find happiness in a new life elsewhere. They are doomed to ever-mounting frustrations. Failure will be the penalty.

The newly arrived missionary immediately faces a host of problems. Language, food, culture, suspicion, boredom, and long, long hours of work are paramount. I can think of no simpler way of illustrating the abrupt change than with the fact that in the Christian world white is the sign of purity, innocence and even happiness; in the Buddhist world it is the sign of death and worn by the mourners. I have heard Westerners say, "That is absolutely ridiculous."

Treatment of animals is something else that brings conflict. When I was a child, my father taught me to love animals. That is the usual procedure among Americans. But in many parts of the world, an animal is nothing more than a beast of burden and a source of food; a dog is only something that guards the house against burglars. I have overheard Chinese say, when an American has cuddled a dog, "That is silly."

All right, who is being ridiculous; who is being silly? The Westerner or the Oriental? It is purely a point of view rooted in people's cultures. Yet, a missionary must graciously learn to understand these customs. After all, a missionary is not a tourist. He is going to live among and work with these people—to be one with them—perhaps for a lifetime. A tourist, on the other hand, stays at the best hotels; eats Western food in the best restaurants if he does not care for the native fare; stays in a country as long as his vacation time permits, or abruptly cuts short his visit and goes elsewhere if he does not find it to his liking. For a tourist, life is simply adjusting to different time zones and being on time for planes and ships.

The missionary has a job to do: devoting his life to God and the spiritual and material welfare of his fellow man. He is poorly paid as against compensation for his skill in a similar profession in the Western world. He works long, long hours and gets no time and a half for overtime after forty hours, as in the United States. He might wash his clothes on a rock by a stream or on a washboard in a pail, as the local people do. There is no such thing as a laundromat and twelve pounds for a quarter.

The missionary eats the local food. As a matter of economics, it is usually all he can afford. Moreover, he should adopt the customs of the local people—to become more like them. Diplomatically, it would be foolhardy to spurn the local hospitality. The food is not at all like what he had back home. Sometimes he finds it delicious; sometimes he cannot stomach it. Yet, if he is going to stay on, he must learn to eat it—and quite often comes to relish it. The change in diet creates still other problems for the missionary. It is often shy of meat because meat is a luxury. Therefore, the diet is low in protein, setting up the possibility of malnutrition. The diet can also have some serious effects on the digestive system. One side effect is diarrhea, sometimes referred to as the Westerner's Disease.

Most rural villages have no American or European movies or stage plays to provide an evening's diversion. Baseball and American football are almost nonexistent. Radio is one of the few entertainment media, but unlike the broadcast band in the United States, there is no flood of local stations, or hi fi, to choose from. Except for an occasional rock-and-roll program, the music is foreign to the newcomers' ears—wailing, sing-song melodies that began to take on meaning only after exhausting listening patience.

The people are generally polite, quite often warm, friendly, generous, companionable, intelligent and hard-working. Some, though, are suspicious of your intentions toward them; they wonder what material benefits the missionary is going to get out of the whole deal. They cannot conceive that the missionary's basic purpose is to give and not receive. The reason is rooted in the fact that, unlike Christianity, the word charity is generally missing from their religions, including Buddhism. There is only one way the missionary can overcome suspicion. He must live his life as a witness of Christ. He must at all times live in a spirit of renunciation, joy, charity, compassion and a sincere interest in the people themselves. He must live by example. I believe wholeheartedly in Father Sun's premise: do not go out on the housetops to preach, or collar people on the streets; let them see the principles of Christianity in practice; let them come to the light of reasoning themselves; let the Holy Spirit have His time to give them the gift of Faith. Wherever he has been, Father Sun has always had converts—not the "rice bowl" Christians, but the true, heart and soul, lifetime converts. The faithful should be counted, not by quantity, but by quality.

When Sister Raphael and I were in the United States, one young school teacher took me aside and wanted to know how she could become a teaching missionary. "I know that I can teach those people much," she said quite sincerely.

"What do you have in mind?" I asked.

"Reading, writing, arithmetic, geography—oh, just all sorts of things."

She did not stand alone in this misconception of those "poor, illiterate" foreigners. It was appalling how knowledge of the world had been misconstrued by ignorance. Taiwan, for instance, has a literacy rate comparable to that of the United States.

Equally disturbing was the teacher's failure to realize that people of other countries could teach her many valuable lessons. Maryann Heim, for instance, said her time spent in Taiwan was a post-graduate course in humanities. Yet, the teacher had lots of company. My attention has been called to zealous missionaries failing simply because they were bent on reshaping everybody and everything around them to their own way of doing things while ignoring the fact that this was often impractical, or contrary to the customs which were good in themselves. It would be impractical, for example, for the missionary doctor to ask the mother to wean her baby at such an early age as is done in the United States. Often the mother's milk is by far the best nourishment the infant will obtain in rural areas of Taiwan, for instance, where cow's milk is not available or too expensive.

Also, it would seem uncalled for to force people to exchange their chopsticks for knife, fork and spoon. How can we say chopsticks are inferior to Western utensils?

I was fortunate in having some knowledge about the

Oriental philosophy of life before going to Taiwan. Still, after my arrival, I learned even more about the virtue of patience and understanding of my fellow man's opinions and customs. The story of the palsied girl, her father and the Chinese New Year taught me much. I could have demanded that the father bring his daughter back each week for a checkup and treatment during the holidays. I might have become upset, angry and sharp in my words at what might seem a callous disrespect on the father's part of the seriousness of her illness. This would be a typical reaction of a Westerner ignoring the fact that the father was simply abiding by a centuries-old belief that seeing a doctor during the New Year season would mean a year of sickness. Nothing would have been gained, and most likely all would have been lost, since the patient would not have come back. Patience and respect for the customs of a people won out, and the patient got well. Such are the things the missionary must weigh when he is dealing with people of another culture.

The language is a problem. Not just one language, but two or more dialects. Missionaries I have known from other parts of the world have told me this is a global matter, and not restricted to just an isolated country here and there. True, interpreters are available. The people soon begin, however, to resent a missionary's using this language crutch. They talk among themselves: "He cannot be very interested in us or he would learn our language." The grapevine carries the word far and wide. To avoid this, to show courtesy, he plunges into daily, hours-long lessons.

After a few months or years in a new country, the missionary discovers that his life can be summed up in one word, monotony. Today is the same as yesterday; tomorrow will be no different. Often he must do the same things each day, seven days a week, and eighteen hours a day. The food is always the same. The people wear the same type of clothing day in and day out. Language lessons become a chore. Inconveniences, such as the outdoor privy or carrying water great distances from the village well, turn into ogres. Lack of tools to work with, such as a delayed shipment of much-needed medicines, and insurmountable problems, such as a patient continually being reinfested by hookworm, develop into nerve-wracking burdens.

All of those problems plus many more—too much work and not enough hours or help to complete it, as an example—face every missionary regardless of whether he is in a lay or religious role. He must learn to forget yesterday; live today; and let tomorrow take care of itself. If he is the type to sit and brood, he is lost. If he is under the spell of a tropical moon, he is likewise lost because the romance quickly becomes tarnished. If he is trying to escape a problem back home, he surely will not last, as he will find new and more complex problems arising from a way of life totally foreign to his upbringing. For that matter, if he is very neurotic, he could become psychotic. That has happened.

The missionary must take up his post with his mind wide open to the fact that he must redesign his own life to fit comfortably within the framework of a different culture while still maintaining his integrity. The missionary comes to serve, not to reap; to give and not receive; to die to self in order to give eternal life to others.